THE AVISSON BOOK OF CONTESTS AND PRIZE COMPETITIONS FOR POETS

AVISSON WRITERS REFERENCE SERIES

THE AVISSON BOOK OF CONTESTS AND PRIZE COMPETITIONS FOR POETS

First Edition, 1997-98

M.L. HESTER, EDITOR

Avisson Press, Inc.
Greensboro

First Edition
Printed in the United States of America

The editor wishes to express his appreciation to Ken White, database editor for the Series, for his help and assistance with this volume.

Library of Congress Cataloging-in-Publication Data

The Avisson book of contests and prize competitions for poets/M.L. Hester, editor. — 1st ed., 1997-98.
    p.   cm. — (Avisson writers reference series)
Includes bibliographical references and index.
ISBN 1-888105-25-9 (lib. bdg.). — ISBN 1-888105-26-7 (pbk.)
1. Literary prizes—United States. I. Hester, M. L. (Martin L.), 1947- . II. Series.
PN171.P75A96   1997
811'.0079—dc21   97-26594
                                                       CIP

Disclaimer: reasonable attempts have been made to ascertain that the information in this book is accurate and timely. However, both the author and publisher specifically disclaim any liability for information that is not. Listing of any prize or competition herein does not constitute an endorsement; users of this volume should use their own judgment with regard to entering or participating in any literary contest or competition.

Contents

INTRODUCTION

In recent years, there has been a sharp increase in the number of contests and prize competitions for poets. These competitions encompass a wide range of subject matter and are sponsored by an equally wide range of magazines and institutions, from prestigious University publishing houses to the very smallest of magazines, edited and produced sometimes by a single individual or a group of part-time volunteers. While this has made it possible for poets to have their work seen and judged by a wider variety of possible publishers (with the potential for wider and more varied audiences for the work, if it wins), at the same time it has made any one contest or competition less important than it might have been in the past.

A number of famous poets (W.S. Merwin and Delmore Schwartz among them) first came to prominence by winning what, at the time, was the most prestigious open competition, the Yale Series of Younger Poets Award. It has been reported that, in those early days, the editors had trouble finding people to enter the contest. This is not the case now. The larger book-manuscript competitions may garner as many as 1,000 entries. Entry fees have risen appropriately; some are $20 or $25. The university press contests have to employ "readers" (usually students) to cull out what they consider the weaker manuscripts. Smaller contests for single poems or chapbooks may only draw 50 or 100 entries, and reading fees may be as low as $3 or $5. But poets are eager to have their work compete.

One might ask, why are there so many contests and competitions? The obvious answer is, to fund the publication of the winning manuscript(s)! Any overflow would go into the coffers of the sponsoring organization. Contests are also a way for new magazines or small literary presses to gain visibility and to attract subscribers and potential contributors. It is a way of saying "we are open for business." But, sadly, while the number of publications is rising, the cost of printing and postage also continues to rise, while what might be called the "hard-core" audience of serious readers/buyers of poetry books or literary magazines has not increased, and may be dwindling. What has *not* dwindled is the number of people who write poetry and wish to have it published. Over the last twenty years, new creative writing programs at colleges and universities have produced thousands of graduates, with more students following behind, each of whom wishes to pursue publication of their work. This may be for personal satisfaction, or in the case of writers with MFA's or Ph.D's, to enable them to find a job, or to advance in the one they have. "Publish or perish" is still very much operative. For that reason, the reader here will find many contests that have an academic flavor, or are connected with a college or university publication. But, an equal number are not.

This book has attempted only to provide the basic information necessary to allow the poet to make up his/her mind about entering a contest, and whether to write for current guidelines. It does not give comprehensive guidelines because they so often change. No phone numbers, fax numbers, or E-mail addresses have been provided here, though some competitions have listed them. Future editions may carry additional information of this sort.

Although every attempt has been made to obtain current and reliable information, poets should not rely solely on the data provided in this book. The sponsoring press or organization should be contacted for full and current guidelines. **Always enclose a #10 self-addressed, stamped envelope when writing for guidelines.**

—— DEFINITION OF TERMS

For the purposes of this book, the terms "contest" and "competition" need to be defined. The two may be used more or less interchangeably, but in general they will refer to a situation where:

1. the writer pays an entry fee, or reading fee, to enter the competition.

2. his/her work is judged on an open and impartial basis by the staff, the editor(s) of the sponsoring publication or organization, and/or a "distinguished judge".

3. the writer has a more or less equal chance to win.

4. The poet is not required to buy a copy of the winning publication. NOTE: "Paid anthologies" have been omitted by the editor whenever a contest is known or suspected to be one. A paid anthology is one which accepts almost any poem, regardless of quality. The poems are then published in an anthology with a hefty retail price. The authors, along with their relatives and friends, are then solicited to buy copies, and usually do. But these are often the only buyers, and the only readers. Paid anthologies are considered to be vanity publications by any serious poet.

Except in a few instances in which the winning poem(s) may be read over the airways, or read as part of a dramatic performance, this volume will concern itself with competitions for print media only; that is, books, chapbooks, or magazines. The editor does not consider the posting of a poem on the Internet, or in some other electronic format, to be "publication" in the usual sense. Hence, any contests for which that is the prize have not been included. (However, some print publications may have an electronic media edition.)

This volume does not attempt to encompass those prizes more properly known as "Awards" (though some contests may call themselves that). An **award** may include an element of competition, but is more often given for work already published, or for an author's lifetime contribution to the arts, etc. Also, awards are often chosen by a select committee from candidates chosen or nominated by the committee or others within the organization, and so is not "open" in the sense that anyone can enter, or that anyone has a chance to win.

Book Competitions have been defined here as those competitions which result in the publication of a book (as opposed to a chapbook), and in which the call for manuscripts asks for work of more than 48 pages. This is a somewhat arbitrary definition, but in some cases the Library of Congress defines a "book" as being 50 pages or more in length. Poetry volumes of lesser length may qualify, however, under their guidelines.

A **chapbook** is a bound volume of less than book length. Chapbooks may be as low as 16, or even fewer, pages. Because of the difficulty of perfect (flatback) binding in these short units, most chapbooks are bound with a process known as saddle-stitching (staples at the spine).

Individual poems are just that, single poems. Note, however, that poems very greatly in length. A poem of more than a few pages may be referred to as a **longpoem**. In fact, longpoems may qualify as a chapbook entry, or even as a book-length manuscript, depending on the contest.

Under these three major categories, contests appear in strict alphabetical order. For instance, a contest entitled The James Francis Zeeman Memorial Competition would be listed under "J". The editor feels this helps to avoid confusion.

An alphabetical listing of all contests, with page numbers, appears in the "Index of Contests." There is also an "Index of Sponsoring Publishers and Organizations," as well as an "Index of Restricted Contests" (see below).

A **distinguished judge** is a poet or critic of some note, who selects the winner of a contest. Many larger contests have a distinguished judge; however, in most cases he or she will not read every entry, but only the top ten or twenty, which are selected beforehand by the editors or other readers.

This volume does not note whether a certain contest will

have a distinguished judge. But the guidelines of various contests may specify this. Having a distinguished judge choose the winner may give a certain contest or competition more prestige, especially in the academic community.

A **blind competition** is one in which the manuscript is sent in without the author's name or other distinguishing marks on the manuscript itself. A cover sheet or entry form identifies the manuscript once it arrives. Generally, an incoming manuscript is assigned a number; the manuscript is then judged on an anonymous basis.

It can easily be seen that this is not a perfect solution. Particularly in the case of major book competitions, paid readers or judges may come across a single poem with which they are familiar, or that is in a style they recognize as that of a particular author. Nevertheless, this form of competition at least tries to be impartial and to give all entrants a fair chance to win.

A **Broadside** is one sheet of paper, which may however be quite large, which is then folded several times to make a booklet or pamphlet. **Leaflets** and **calendars** are other forms of publication.

The terms **entry fee** and **reading fee** are used more or less interchangeably. This is a fee paid to the sponsoring body of the competition by the author, for reading his/her work and as a condition of entering the contest or competition. Not all contests have entry fees; some sponsored by foundations or other organizations do not need or require them.

——Symbols Used

This symbol ◆ denotes a contest that is open only to members of a certain group or class of poets (for instance, African-Americans, people living west of the Mississippi

River, etc.) It has also been used here to denote a contest which is open only to poets without a previous book publication, or, alternatively, one open only to those who have published a previous book. The editor has chosen to call these **restricted competitions**, because they are not open to everyone. Wherever possible, *necessary qualifications for writers in restricted competitions are placed in italics.*

Certain prizes which encompass **Grants, Fellowships, Residencies** or **Mentors,** but which have a competitive element, have been included in this book. This symbol ● appears at the beginning of any listing so denoted. Many of these contests are also in the "restricted" category.

Deadlines: in most cases, the given deadline for entries refers to the date at which the manuscript or entry arrives at the office of the sponsor. However, in some instances a deadline may refer to the date the manuscript is postmarked. Always check the current guidelines to make sure.

The deadlines given here are for the most recent contest, or that appear on the most recent guidelines sheet or announcement available; however, deadlines very often change from year to year, or may even be extended after a contest is announced.

Poets are strongly urged and advised to write for current guidelines in all cases. Deadlines and entry fees vary frequently. Many contests change rules and requirements each time a contest is run. Some competitions simply cease to operate, or the sponsoring publication goes out of print. Following the **guidelines** provided by the sponsoring organization is the single most important thing a poet can do to ensure that his/her work is read and given every opportunity to win. Guidelines may be simple, or complicated and time-consuming to follow. Some contests may require two or more copies of the work submitted, or biographical information, etc. Some require a properly filled- out **entry form** provided by the sponsor. In any case, the poet needs to read and follow the provided guidelines.

A sample guidelines sheet follows.

AVISSON PRESS POETRY BOOK COMPETITION
Guidelines

1. Manuscripts should be from 50 to 80 pages in length, typewritten or word-processed (either single or double spaced), on standard size white paper. Clear photocopies or printouts are acceptable.

2. There are no restrictions as to subject matter or style.

3. Original poetry only; no translations or collections written by more than one author will be accepted.

4. Simultaneous submissions are permitted; but, in the case of a manuscript accepted for publication elsewhere, the poet should notify Avisson Press immediately. A poet may submit more than one manuscript; however, each should include the entry fee.

5. The poet's name or other identification should not be on the manuscript pages themselves; a "cover sheet" should be added with the poet's name, address, and phone number; he or she may add a bio or publications/credit sheet as well.

6. Poems previously published in magazines, anthologies and/or limited edition chapbooks are acceptable for inclusion. The poet should retain the rights to the work.

7. A non-refundable handling fee of $12.00 made payable to Avisson Press should accompany the manuscript; include letter-sized SASE for notification of the winning manuscript. All entrants submitting a manuscript will receive, if they desire, at no extra charge a copy of the winning book, when published. No manuscripts will be returned, but will be recycled after the winner has been chosen. The poet may also include a self-addressed postcard for notification of receipt of the manuscript. Entrants should notify the Press of any change of address.

8. All entries should be postmarked by June 15, 1998. *The competition is held only in even-numbered years.*
9. The Press will assume no responsibility for lost or damaged manuscripts. Poets should retain a copy for their protection.
10. The winning entry will be announced by September 15, 1998. The winning manuscript will be chosen by the staff of Avisson Press, or by a distinguished judge. The decision of the editor or the judge will be final. The winning manuscript will be published within six months in a trade paperback edition, sent to appropriate review sources, and added to the Avisson catalogue. Announcement of the winner will be made in the appropriate newsletters and other media.
11. Manuscripts and correspondence should be sent to: Avisson Press, Inc., 3007 Taliaferro Road, Greensboro, North Carolina 27408.

—— PUTTING YOUR BEST FOOT FORWARD

1. Always follow the contest guidelines as closely as possible.
2. If you are submitting the same manuscript to more than one contest or competition, and one is a "blind" competition that does not allow your name and address to show on the manuscript, do not simply take an old photocopy and use "white-out" or some other preparation to cover it up, or place a blank label over it. This says very loudly that you are lazy and don't particularly care what the contest editors think. It also gives them the impression that you are entering many contests with the same manuscript.
3. You may send manuscripts by "special 4th class, manuscript rate," but if you do so, please note that it might take several weeks to arrive. First class or priority mail is faster, safer, and makes a better impression. It is also more expensive, and you may have to weigh cost versus the other benefits. Some contests may require you to send only by first class mail.
4. Sending your manuscripts by registered or certified mail is permissible, but it may irk some editors, especially if they are not in the office to sign for it when the first delivery attempt is

made, and they have to trundle up to the post office to retrieve a notice, perhaps thinking it is an important legal paper or notice of eviction, etc. Registered or certified mail also takes more time to get there, and may not be worth the bother. Enclosing a self-addressed postcard is a cheaper and better way of making sure your manuscript has reached its destination. Type or print on the back of the card something like "Received by" and "date". Write the name of the contest somewhere on the card, or add a code which will let you know where your postcard is being returned from.

Some writers occasionally send manuscripts by UPS or other express services; in general this is not necessary, unless time is very short or you want a guaranteed delivery.

BOOK COMPETITIONS

Prize Competitions *for Poets*

◆AGNES LYNCH STARRETT POETRY PRIZE. $2,500 and book publication. *For US poets who have not yet published a full length poetry book* (48+ pages). $12.50 entry fee. Submit only in March or April. Agnes Lynch Starrett Poetry Prize, University of Pittsburgh Press, 127 N. Bellefield Avenue, Pittsburgh, PA 15260.

AKRON POETRY PRIZE. Prize: book publication. Submit poetry manuscripts of 60-100 pages. Send only between May 15 and June 30. Entry fee: $15. University of Akron Press, Akron Poetry Prize, 374B Bierce Library, University of Akron, Akron, OH 44325-1703.

◆THE ALICE FAY DI CASTAGNOLA AWARD. For a poetry manuscript-in-progress. *Open only to members of the Poetry Society of America.* $1,000 prize; December 22 deadline. Write for complete guidelines to: Alice Fay Di Castagnola Award, Poetry Society of America, 15 Gramercy Park, New York, NY 10003.

ANHINGA PRIZE FOR POETRY. $2,000 and book publication. For a manuscript of original poetry by a poet who has published no more than one full length collection (48 pages or more). Submit manuscript of 48-72 pages, only one poem per page. Include two SASEs. $20 reading fee; deadline March 15. Anhinga Press, PO Box 10595, Tallahassee, FL 32302.

◆AMERICAN POETRY REVIEW/HONICKMAN FIRST BOOK PRIZE. Prize: $3,000 and publication. *For a first book of poetry.* Submit between August 1 and October 31 (postmark). $20 entry fee. Write for complete guidelines. APR/Honickman First Book Prize, *The American Poetry Review,* 17212 Walnut Street, Philadelphia, PA 19103.

◆ARKANSAS POETRY AWARD. *For a US poet without previous book publication*; submit manuscript of 50-80 pages. Is blind competition. $15 reading fee; May 1 deadline. Arkansas

Poetry Award, University of Arkansas Press, 201 Ozark Avenue, Fayetteville, AK 72701.

ASSOCIATED WRITING PROGRAMS AWARD SERIES IN POETRY, SHORT FICTION, THE NOVEL, AND CREATIVE NON-FICTION. The winning works will appear through prearranged agreements with four university presses; AWP acts as a literary agent to try to place finalists' manuscripts. Authors will receive a standard royalty from books sold. A $2,000 honorarium is given in each category every year. Submissions: postmark of January 1 through February 28 only. There is a $15 nonmember, and $10 AWP member reading and handling fee. Send an SASE for complete guidelines. AWP Award Series, Tallwood House, MS-1E3, George Mason University, Fairfax, VA 22030.

AVISSON PRESS POETRY BOOK COMPETITION. Book publication in trade paperback edition. Prize: $150 and 100 copies of book. Send 50-80 page manuscript. Poetry may be previously published in magazines or chapbooks. Is blind competition. Reading/entry fee $15. Submit in even-numbered years only (next competition is 1998). June 15 deadline. Editor, Avisson Press, Inc., 3007 Taliaferro Road, Greensboro, NC 27408.

BALCONES POETRY PRIZE. For poetry books in English of 42 pages or more. $500 prize. $15 reading fee. December 15 deadline. Austin Community College,. Balcones Poetry Prize, Northridge Campus, 11928 Stonehollow Drive, Austin, TX 78758.

◆BARNARD NEW WOMEN POETS PRIZE. *Open only to women poets who have not yet published a book-length volume of poetry.* Prize: $1,000 and book publication.No entry fee listed; October 15 deadline. Send for complete guidelines: Barnard New Women Poets Prize, Barnard College, 3009 Broadway, New York, NY 10027.

BEATRICE HAWLEY AWARD. For a book-length manuscript of

poetry. Prize is 100 copies of published book. $15 reading fee; January 15 deadline. Write for full details to alicejamesbooks, 98 Main Street, Farmington, ME 04938.

BLUESTEM AWARD. For a book length collection of poems by a US author. $1,000 cash prize plus publication. Submit manuscript of original poetry of at least 48 pages. $15 reading fee; March 3 deadline. The Bluestem Award, English Department, Emporia State University, Emporia, KS 66801.

BRITTINGHAM PRIZE IN POETRY. For a book length manuscript of poetry. $1,000 prize and book publication by the University of Wisconsin Press. Submit manuscript of 50-80 pages. $15 reading fee; submit between September 1 and October 1. Write for guidelines to Series Editor, University of Wisconsin Press, 114 N. Murray Street, Madison, WI 53715.

◆CAPRICORN BOOK AWARDS. Includes poetry. *For a manuscript of original poetry of 48-68 pages in length by a poet over the age of forty.* $1,000 prize plus public reading. $15 reading fee; December 31 deadline. Send for guidelines and entry form. The Writer's Voice of the West Side YMCA, 5 West 63rd Street, New York, NY 10023.

CESAR VELLEJO PRIZE. For a book-length manuscript of original poetry in English by a single author. Write for complete guidelines including deadlines and entry/reading fees. Pacific International, Box 250, Davis, CA 95617-0250.

COLORADO PRIZE. For a book-length manuscript of poetry. Prize: $1,000 and book publication. $20 reading fee. Write for deadlines. Colorado Prize, Colorado Review, English Department, Colorado State University, Fort Collins, CO 80523.

CLEVELAND STATE UNIVERSITY POETRY CENTER PRIZE. $1,000 plus book publication. For book-length (50-100 pages) manuscript of poetry. $15 reading fee; Submit December 1-March 1. "The Poetry Center also expects to publish one or more of the runners-up for the prize competiton in the CSU Poetry Series." Send for guidelines to: Poetry Center Prize, English Department, RT 1815, 1983 E. 24th Steet, Cleveland State University, Cleveland, OH 44115.

EATON LITERARY ASSOCIATES LITERARY AWARDS. For a book-length manuscript. Includes poetry. The prize: $2,500. August 31 deadline. Eaton Literary Associates Literary Awards, Eaton Literary Agency, Box 49795, Sarasota, FL 34230-6795.

THE EMILY CLARK BALCH AWARDS. Includes poetry. $500 for the best poem appearing annually in the *Virginia Quarterly Review* literary magazine. Submissions only as submissions to magazine. *Virginia Quarterly Review*, One West Range, Charlottesville, VA 22903.

FELIX POLLAK PRIZE IN POETRY. For a book-length manuscript of poetry. $1,000 prize and book publication by University of Wisconsin Press. Submit manuscript of 50-80 pages. $15 reading fee; submit between September 1-October 1. Write for guidelines to Series Editor, University of Wisconsin Press, 114 N. Murray Street, Madison, WI 53715.

FIRST INTERNATIONAL POETRY AWARDS. $2,000 first prize, $1,000 second prize, $500 third prize, other awards; and publication. For poetry manuscripts of 32 pages or more. Awards are granted to different nationalities (U.S., British, Australia/New Zealand) in alternate years. Write for entry fees and deadlines: Abbey National, P.L.C., First International Poetry Awards, Cleveland Arms Building, Suite 4-E, 205 West 95 Street, New York, NY 10025.

◆FIRST SERIES AWARD . Includes poetry. *For a poet who has never published a full-length work of poetry.* Prize: $1,000 as advance against royalties. Submit manuscripts of at least 65 pages in length. $10 reading fee; submit between October 1-February 1. Mid-List Press, 4324 12th Avenue, South Minneapolis, MN 55407.

◆FOUR WAY BOOKS AWARD SERIES. *For a US poet who has previously published one or more books of poetry.* Prize of $2,000 plus book publication, plus opportunities for readings. $15 entry fee; deadline, postmark by May 4. Four Way Books, P.O. Box 535, Village Station, NY 10014.

◆FOUR WAY BOOKS INTRO SERIES. *For a book length manuscript of poetry by a US author who has not published a book of poetry.* $1,500 plus book publication, readings. $15 entry fee. Deadline, postmark by May 4. Four Way Books, P.O. Box 535, Village Station, NY 10014.

GARDEN STREET PRESS POETRY PRIZE. For a book-length manuscript of poetry, 48 to 68 pages. Prize of 100 copies of the published book and publication. $15 reading fee; June 30 deadline. Garden Street Press, P.O. Box 1231, Truro, MA 02666.

◆IOWA POETRY PRIZES. $1,000 and book publication by the University of Iowa Press. Two manuscripts are selected. *Open to any writer who has published at least one book of poems* (50 pages or more in an edition of 500 copies). No reading fee. Submit in February and March only. University of Iowa Press, Iowa Poetry Prize, 119 West Park Road, 100 Kuhl House, Iowa City, IA 52242.

◆JAMES D. PHELAN LITERARY AWARDS. *For writers born in California, who are 20-35 years old.* For unpublished works in progress: a poetry collection. Two prizes of $2,000 each. January 31 deadline. San Francisco Foundation, Intersection for the Arts, 446 Valencia St., San Francisco CA 94103.

◆JOSEPH HENRY JACKSON LITERARY AWARDS. *Nevada and Northern California writers only, 20-35 years old.* For unpublished works in progress: a poetry collection. Two prizes: $2,000 each. January 31 deadline. San Francisco Foundation, Intersection for the Arts, 446 Valencia St., San Francisco, CA 94103.

JUNIPER PRIZE. $1,000 prize awarded annually. In odd-numbered years the prize is awarded for a poet's first book; in even-numbered years, the prize is awarded for a second book or subsequent books. Submit book-length manuscript of poetry. $10 reading fee; September 30 deadline. Write for guidelines: Juniper Prize, University of Massachusetts Press, University of Massachusetts, Amherst, MA 01003.

◆KATHERINE BAKELESS NASON PRIZES. Includes poetry. *For writers who have not previously published a book.* Prize: book publication and fellowship. Send poetry manuscript of approximately 50 pages. $10 reading fee; March 1 deadline. Bakeless Prizes, c/o Bread Loaf Writers' Conference, Middlebury College, Middlebury, VT 05753

KATHRYN A. MORTON PRIZE IN POETRY. $2,000 and book publication. Manuscripts should be at least 48 pages in length. Submit between January 1 and February 15. Send for required entry form and guidelines. Poetry Prize, Sarabande Books, 2234 Dundee Road, Suite 200, Louisville, KY 40205.

KATE TUFTS DISCOVERY AWARD. For "a first or very early work by a poet of genuine promise." Prize: $5,000. Work submitted must be either a published book or an unpublished book-length manuscript. "In the case of an unpublished work, the entry must provide evidence that the poet has previously been published in a legitimate book, magazine, or literary journal." Entry form required. No fee listed. September 15 postmark deadline. Kate Tufts Poetry Awards, The Claremont Graduate School, 740 N. College Avenue, Claremont, CA 91711.

Prize Competitions *for Poets*

KENNETH PATCHEN COMPETITION IN THE GENRE OF POETRY. For a full-length manuscript of poetry. The prize in poetry is given in odd-numbered years. Prize: $100, book publication and 50 copies of the published book. $10 reading fee; October 31 deadline. Write: The Patchen Competition, Pig Iron Press, PO Box 237, Youngstown, OH 44501.

KINGSLEY TUFTS POETRY AWARD. For "a work by an emerging poet, one who is past the very beginning but has not yet reached the acknowledged pinnacle of his or her career." Prize: $50,000. Work submitted must be either a published book or an unpublished book-length manuscript. "In the case of an unpublished work, the entry must provide evidence that the poet has previously been published in a legitimate book, magazine, or literary journal." Entry form required. No fee listed. September 15 postmark deadline. Kingsley Tufts Poetry Awards, The Claremont Graduate School, 740 N. College Avenue, Claremont, CA 91711.

LA JOLLA POETS PRESS "NATIONAL POETRY SERIES" AWARD. $500 and publication for a poetry manuscript of 60-70 pages in length. $10 reading fee; October 1 deadline. Kathleen Iddings, editor, La Jolla Poets Press, National Poetry Series Award, P.O. Box 8638, La Jolla, CA 92038.

LARRY LEVIS POETRY PRIZE. Prize: $2,000 and publication of a full-length poetry collection. Submit manuscripts of any length. Entry fee: $15. Deadline: April 30. Four Way Books, P.O. Box 535, Village Station, New York, NY 10014.

MARIANNE MOORE POETRY PRIZE. For original, unpublished poetry manuscript of 48 pages or more. $1,000 prize and publication plus participation in readings. Is blind competition. $15 entry fee; April 30 deadline. Helicon Nine Editions, 3607 Pennsylvania Street, Kansas City, MO 64111.

◆MARYLAND-TOWSON STATE UNIVERSITY PRIZE FOR LITERATURE.

Including poetry. *For writers under 40 years of age with at least 3 years state residency.* The prize: $1,000. Submit book-length manuscript. May 15 deadline. Towson State University, College of Liberal Arts, Towson, MD 21204-7097.

MASTERS LITERARY AWARD. Grand prize of $1,000 and publication with Center Press. $15 reading fee per entry. Deadline: ongoing. Write for complete guidelines to: Center Press, PO Box 16452, Encino, CA 91416.

◆MINNESOTA VOICES PROJECT COMPETITION. *For poets and prose writers, unpublished commercially, who reside in Iowa, Minnesota, North Dakota, South Dakota, or Wisconsin.* Prizes to 3 poets: $500 each and publication by New Rivers Press. April 1 deadline. New Rivers Press, Minnesota Voices Project, 420 North 5 St., #910, Minneapolis, MN 55401.

◆NAOMI LONG MADGETT POETRY AWARD. *Open to African-American writers only.* Prize: $500 plus book publication by Michigan State University Press. Submit manuscript of 60-80 pages in length between February 1 and April 1. Lotus Press, Inc., P.O. Box 21607, Detroit, Michigan 48221.

◆NATALIE ORNISH POETRY AWARD. *For the best book of poetry by a member of a Texas poetry association.* The prize: $1,000. January 4 deadline. Natalie Ornish Poetry Award, The Texas Institute of Letters, Box 9032, Wichita Falls, TX 76308

NATIONAL POETRY SERIES OPEN COMPETITION. For a book-length poetry manuscript. The prizes: five $1,000 awards and publication by a university or small press. $25 entry fee; January1-February 15 submission dates. National Poetry Series Open Competition, National Poetry Series, Box G, Hopewell, NJ 08525.

NEW AMERICAN POETRY COMPETITION. For a full-length manuscript of poetry. Is blind competition. $25 reading fee. Submit at any time. Sun & Moon Press, 6026 Wilshire Boulevard, Los Angeles, CA 90036.

◆NEW ENGLAND 96 INC./ BRUCE ROSSLEY LITERARY AWARD. For "unknown" poetry or fiction writers of outstanding merit: *Connecticutt, Maine, Massachusetts, New Hampshire, Rhode Island,Vermont residency required.* The prize: $1,000. Nominations only , August 1-September 30. Submit 6 copies of a published book or unpublished manuscript of poetry. Write for full details and guidelines. 96 Inc., Box 15559, Boston, MA 02215.

◆NEW ISSUES PRESS FIRST BOOK POETRY PRIZE. $1,000 prize and publication. Submit 48-64 pages of poems, a brief bio, publication credits if any, SAS postcard and envelope for notification and $10 fee. *Only poets who have not published a full-length collection of poems are eligible.* Send entries to: Herbert Scott, Editor, New Issues Press Poetry Series, Western Michigan University, Kalamazoo, MI 49008-5092.

◆NEW MUSE AWARD. *For book manuscripts of 50-65 pages in length from a poet who has not yet published a book-length collection of poetry.* Prize: publication. Entry fee of $15; March 31 deadline. Write: Broken Jaw Press, Box 596 Station A, Fredricton, New Brunswick E3B 5A6 Canada.

◆NEW WOMEN POETS PRIZE. $500 and publication by Beacon Press. *Awarded to a woman poet who has not published a full-length poetry collection.* Submit two copies of a book-length manuscript between 50-100 pages. Oct. 15 deadline. Send SASE. Barnard College, New Women Poets Prize, Columbia University, 3009 Broadway, New York, NY 10027-6598.

NEW YORK UNIVERSITY PRESS PRIZE FOR POETRY. For a book-length manuscript of poetry. $1,000 honorarium and book publication by New York University Press. Is blind competition. Submit manuscript with one-page letter of support (on letterhead) from "qualified reader"—editor, agent, teacher, etc.. No reading fee listed; May 2 deadline. The New York University Press Prizes, Attn: Poetry, c/o New York University Press, 70 Washington Square South, New York, NY 10012.

◆NICHOLAS ROERICH POETRY PRIZE. *For poets who have not yet published a full-length volume.* Prizes: $1,000 first prize; second prize, full scholarship to the Wesleyan Writers Conference, Middleton, CT. Is blind competition. Manuscripts should be original poetry of at least 48 pages in length. $15 reading fee; October 15 deadline. Story Line Press, Three Oaks Farm, Brownsville, OR 97327.

◆NORTH AMERICAN NATIVE AUTHORS FIRST BOOK AWARDS. Including poetry. *American Indian, Aleut, Inuit or Metis ancestry required.* The prize: $500 and publication by Greenfield Review Press. Submit 64-100 pages of poetry. January 15-March 1 submission dates. Native Writers Circle of the Americas, North American Native Authors First Book Awards, Greenfield Review Literary Center, Box 308, Two Middle Grove Rd., Greenfield Center, NY 12633.

NORTHWOODS JOURNAL NATIONAL POETRY COMPETITION . VFor a book-length work of poetry. First prize: $250 as advance against royalties and publication of winning manuscript as a book; other prizes, $150, $100. Is blind competition. Entry fee $12 for up to 128 page manuscript; over 128 pages, $24. January 15 deadline. Write for complete guidelines to: Contest Editor, *Northwoods Journal*, PO Box 298, Thomaston, ME 04861.

OHIO STATE UNIVERSITY PRESS/THE JOURNAL AWARD IN POETRY. For full-length manuscript of poetry. The prize: publication by Ohio State University Press plus $1,000 in addition to royalties. Submit manuscripts of 48 pages or more, original poetry only. Reading fee of $15. Submit only during the month of September (no later than September 30 postmark). David Citino, Poetry Editor, The Ohio State University Press, 180 Pressey Hall, 1070 Carmack Road, Columbus, OH 43210.

OMMATION PRESS BOOK CONTEST. Includes poetry. The prize: book publication and 100 copies. December 31 deadline. Write for full guidelines: Ommation Book Contest, 5548 N. Sawyer, Chicago, IL 60625.

OWL CREEK POETRY PRIZE. $750 prize and book publication. Submit manuscript of at least 50 pages in length. $10 entry fee; February 15 deadline. Send for guidelines: Owl Creek Poetry Prize, Owl Creek Press, 1620 N. 45th St., Seattle, WA 98103.

P.L.C. INTERNATIONAL POETRY AWARDS. Open to U.S. poets every third year (1996-1999, etc.), for the best book-length poetry manuscript. The prize: $2,000. Submit a manuscript of 32 pages of poetry. Deadline to be announced in 1998-9. Abbey National, P.L.C. International Poetry Awards, Cleveland Arms Building, 4-E, 205 W. 95th St., New York, NY 10025-6383.

PEREGRINE SMITH POETRY COMPETITION. $500 and book publication. Submit a 64-page manuscript of poetry. $15 reading fee. Submit during the month of April only. Gibbs Smith, Publisher, Peregrine Smith Poetry Competition, P.O. Box 667, Layton, UT 84041.

QUARTERLY REVIEW OF LITERATURE POETRY BOOK SERIES. For a book-length manuscript, 50-100 pages; a long poem, a play in verse or poetry, or poetry translation is also eligible. The series publishes 5 manuscripts annually. $1,000 prize plus 100 copies and book publication. Submit only during May or November. *Quarterly Review of Literature*, 26 Haslet Avenue, Princeton, NJ 08450.

THE RICHARD J. MARGOLIS AWARD, of $1,000, is given annually to a poet, essayist, or journalist "whose work recalls Richard J. Margolis's warmth, humor, and concern for social issues." To nominate a writer, send three copies of at least two samples of the writer's work, published or unpublished, of no more than thirty pages, and a short biographical note. Deadline: July 1. Apply to: Richard J. Margolis Award, 101 Arch Street, 9th Floor, Boston, MA 02110, Attention: Harry S. Margolis.

◆THE ROANOKE-CHOWAN AWARD FOR POETRY. *North Carolina residents only*—3 years residence by July 1, year of contest. The prize: a cup. Submit book-length poetry manuscript. July 15 deadline. The Roanoke-Chowan Award for Poetry, North Carolina Literary & Historical Association, 109 E. Jones St., Raleigh, NC 27601-2807.

SAMUEL FRENCH MORSE POETRY PRIZE. For a first or second book of poetry. $500 prize and book publication. $10 reading fee; September 15 deadline. Morse Prize, English Department, Northeastern University, 406 Holmes Hall Boston, MA 02115.

◆THE SANDEEN & SULLIVAN PRIZES (ERNEST SANDEEN PRIZE IN POETRY). For a book length manuscript of poetry by an author who has published at least one previous book of poetry. $500 prize plus publication. Poetry manuscripts are read only in odd-numbered years. August 1 deadline. Send for complete guidelines: The Sandeen/Sullivan Prizes, Department of English, University of Notre Dame, Notre Dame, IN 46556.

SILVERFISH REVIEW—GERALD CABLE POETRY BOOK CONTEST. For a 64-80 page manuscript of poetry. $1,000 prize plus 25 copies of the published book. For guidelines and application form write: Silverfish Review Press, P.O. Box 3541, Eugene, OR 97403.

◆STAN & TOM WICK POETRY PRIZE. *For a first book of poems*; prize of $1,000 and book publication. May 1 deadline. Write for complete guidelines to: Poetry Prize, Kent State University Press, PO Box 5190, Kent, OH 44242-0001.

Prize Competitions *for Poets*

T.S. Eliot Prize. Prize: $1,500 and publication of the winning manuscript. For a book-length collection of poetry. Is blind competition. Submit manuscript of 64-96 pages. $25 reading fee; October 31 deadline. T.S. Eliot Prize, Thomas Jeferson University Press, MCIIIL 100 East Normal Street, Kirksville, MO 63501.

Urthona Press competition. For a poetry manuscript of at least 60 pages in length. $10 reading fee; September 30 deadline. Urthona Press, 34 Wall Street, No. 708, Asheville, NC 28801.

◆The Utah Arts Council has awards of up to $1,000 available for book-length collections of poetry, or for single poems. *Open to Utah residents only.* Send for information to: Literature Division, Utah Arts Council, 617 East South Temple Street, Salt Lake City, Utah 84102.

◆Utah Original Writing Competition . Includes poetry. *Open only to Utah residents.* Prize: $5,000 payment to publisher to subsidize publication of the winning entry as a book. Poetry prize available once in four years (alternates with awards for novel, juvenile literature, and nonfiction). June 15 deadline. Write for guidelines to: Literary Competition Division, Utah Arts Council, 617 East South Temple Street, Salt Lake City, UT 84102.

Vassar Miller Prize in Poetry. $500 prize and book publication. Manuscripts should be 50-80 pages in length. For guidelines, deadlines and fees, contact: Vassar Miller Prize in Poetry, c/o English Department, Old Dominion University, Norfolk, VA 23529.

Verna Emery Poetry Prize. Prize: book publication by Purdue University Press. Is blind competition. Submit poetry manuscript of 60-90 pages in length. $10 entry fee; April 15 postmark deadline. Verna Emery Poetry Prize, Purdue University Press, 1532 South Campus Courts—E,

West Lafayette, Indiana 47907.

VIOLET HAAS REED POETRY PRIZE. $500 prize, 50 copies of the book and publication. Submit manuscript of 50-75 pages. $10 entry fee; January 15 deadline. Snake Nation Press, 110 #2 West Force, Valdosta, GA 31601.

◆THE WALT WHITMAN AWARD. *For a book-length manuscript by a poet who has not previously published a volume of poetry.* $1,000 prize and publication by an independent publisher. The Academy of American Poets purchases several thousand copies of the book to distribute among its members. Entry form required. $20 reading fee; submit between September 15-November 15. Write for complete guidelines. The Walt Whitman Award, The Academy of American Poets, 584 Broadway, Suite 1208, New York, NY 10012

WASHINGTON PRIZE BOOK COMPETITION. $1,000 prize plus publication. Submit manuscript of 48-64 pages. $15 reading fee; submit between February 1 and March 1. The Word Works Washington Prize, P.O. Box 42164, Washington, DC 20015.

WHITE PINE PRESS POETRY PRIZE. For a manuscript of 48-96 pages by a U.S. author. Prize of $500 and book publication. $15 reading fee; December 1 deadline. Write for complete guidelines to: Poetry Prize, White Pine Press, 10 Village Square, Fredonia, NY 14063.

WINTHROP UNIVERSITY POETRY AWARD. For book manuscripts. Submit 90-120 page manuscript (double spaced). $10 reading fee. Write for complete guidelines, including deadlines and entry/reading fees. Poetry contest, Department of English, Winthrop University, Rock Hill, SC 29733.

ANISFIELD-WOLF BOOK AWARDS. $5,000 prize. Is annual award. For a poetry volume "that has made a contribution to our understanding of racism." Deadline: January 31. The Cleveland Foundation, Avisfield-Wolf Book Awards, Suite 1400, Hanna Building, 1422 Euclid Avenue, Cleveland, OH 44115.

WOMEN-IN-LITERATURE POETRY MANUSCRIPT CONTEST. For poets who have published no more than one previous full-length book of poetry. $600 cash prize plus book publication. Submit manuscript of 50-75 pages. $20 reading fee; submit between January 1 and March 15. Women-in-Literature Inc., P.O. Box 60550, Reno, NV 89506.

WRITER'S DIGEST NATIONAL SELF-PUBLISHED BOOK AWARDS. For self-published book of poetry in an edition of 500 copies or more. The author must have paid the full cost of production or publication for the book. Overall first-place winner (for all categories) receives $1,000 and promotion in *Writer's Digest* magazine. Other awards of $250 each. Entry form required. $95 judging fee; December 15 deadline. For information contact: Writer's Digest National Self-Publishing Awsrds, 1507 Dana Avenue, Cincinnati, OH 45207.

◆YALE SERIES OF YOUNGER POETS COMPETITION. *For a US poet under the age of 40 who has not yet published a book of poetry.* The Prize: book publication by Yale University Press. Submit manuscript of 48-64 pages. $15 reading fee. Submissions accepted during February only. Yale Series of Younger Poets, Yale University Press, P.O. Box 209040, New Haven, CT 06520.

POETRY CHAPBOOK CONTESTS

Prize Competitions *for Poets*

ACORN-RUKEYSER CHAPBOOK CONTEST. For manuscript up to 30 pages in length. Poetry should exemplify the "People's Poetry" tradition, as in the work of Muriel Rukeyser and Milton Acorn. $100 prize plus publication. October 31 deadline. Acorn-Rukeyser Chapbook Contest, c/o Unfinished Monument Press, P.O. Box 4279, Pittsburgh, PA 15203.

BACCHAE PRESS CHAPBOOK CONTEST. Prize of 50 copies of book. Send 16-24 page manuscript, bio sheet and acknowledgment page. $8 reading fee. Bacchae Press, c/o Brown Financial Group, #10 Sixth Street, Suite 101, Astoria, OR 97103.

◆BEAR STAR PRESS POETRY CONTEST. $500 prize, plus 50 copies of the published chapbook. Open only to women in the Western U.S. Submit manuscript of 20-50 pages. $12 reading fee. Write for complete guidelines and deadlines to: Bear Star Press, 185 Hollow Oak Drive, Cohasset, CA 95973.

◆BLACFAX POETRY CHAPBOOK SERIES. Series of chapbooks by African-American writers. Send for complete guidelines including deadlines and entry/reading fees. Blacfax, Midtown Station, P.O. Box 542, New York, NY 10018.

CENTER FOR BOOK ARTS POETRY CHAPBOOK COMPETITION. $500 prize and publication. Submit manuscript of 16-24 pages or one long poem (see line limit). $10 entry fee. December 31 deadline. Center For Book Arts, 626 Broadway, 5th floor, New York, NY 10012.

CLEVELAND STATE UNIVERSITY POETRY CENTER PRIZE (CHAPBOOKS). Prize is publication. For chapbook-length (20-50pages) manuscript of poetry. $10 reading fee; Submit December 1-March 1. Send for guidelines to: Poetry Center Prize, English Department, RT 1815, 1983 E. 24th Steet, Cleveland State University, Cleveland, OH 44115.

COREOPSIS POETRY CHAPBOOK COMPETITION. For 20-30 page

manuscript. $100 prize plus 100 copies of book. $9 entry fee. Send for complete guidelines. Open deadline. Coreopsis Books, 1384 Township Drive, Lawrenceville, GA 30243.

DANCING WORDS PRESS POETRY CHAPBOOK SERIES. Submit manuscript of 16-32 pages. Payment/prize in copies of published book. $5 reading fee; open deadline. Dancing Words Press, Chapbook Submissions, 449 Ninth Street, Gretna, LA 70053.

DEAD METAPHOR PRESS CHAPBOOK CONTEST. For poetry manuscript up to 24 pages in length; prose manuscripts of similar length may also be submitted. $8 entry fee; October 31 deadline. Dead Metaphor Press, PO Box 2076, Boulder, CO 80306-2076.

DEFINED PROVIDENCE CHAPBOOK CONTEST. Write for complete guidelines including deadlines and entry/reading fees. Chapbook contest, *Defined Providence*, 26 E. Fort Lee Road, #2B, Bogota, NJ 07603.

DEVIL'S MILLHOPPER POETRY CHAPBOOK CONTEST. Prize of $50 plus 50 copies of finished book. Submit manuscript of up to 24 pages of poetry. $10 reading fee; submit between January 1-February 28. Write for guidelines: The Devil's Millhopper Press, University of South Carolina-Aiken, 171 University Parkway, Aiken, South Carolina 29801.

FIRELANDS WRITING CENTER POETRY CHAPBOOK CONTEST. Prize: $100 and publication. Submit 10-12 pages of poetry on single theme, or comprising a unified whole. $10 reading fee; June 5 deadline. Write for guidelines to: *The Heartlands Today*, Firelands Writing Center, Firelands College of BGSU, Huron, OH 44839.

FRANK CAT PRESS CHAPBOOK COMPETITION. For a manuscript of 20-24 pages in length. $7 reading fee; March 1 deadline.

Submit to: The Frank Cat Press, 1008 Ouray Ave., Grand Junction, CO 81501.

FRANK O'HARA AWARD CHAPBOOK COMPETITION. $200 Prize and 25 copies plus publication. For a "small collection" of poetry. $10 reading fee, each collection; February 1 deadline. *Thorngate Road* magazine, Campus Box 4240, Department of English, Illinois State University, Normal, IL 61790.

GERALD CABLE POETRY CHAPBOOK CONTEXT. Send for complete guidelines including deadlines and entry/reading fees. Write *Silverfish Review* Press, PO Box 3541, Eugene, OR 97403.

GREEN LAKE CHAPBOOK PRIZE. For a poetry manuscript under 40 pages in length. $500 prize plus publication and advance against royalties. $10 entry fee; August 15 deadline. Owl Creek Press, 1620 North 45th Street, Seattle, WA 98103.

HEAVEN BONE PRESS INTERNATIONAL CHAPBOOK COMPETITION. For 30 page manuscript of poetry. $10 reading fee; July 30 deadline. Write Heaven Bone Press, PO Box 486, Chester, NY 10918.

HYPER-ALLERGENIC CHAPBOOK CONTEST. Write for complete guidelines including deadlines and entry/reading fees. Proper PH Publications, Pam Hartney, 1659 23rd Street, Cuyahoga Falls, OH 44223-1001.

I.E. MAGAZINE POETRY CHAPBOOK CONTEST. For a chapbook-length manuscript. $50 first prize plus 10 copies of anthology. Reading fee $10. May 31 deadline. *IE* Magazine, P.O. Box 73403, Houston, TX 77273.

ILLINOIS WRITERS INC. CHAPBOOK CONTEST. For manuscript of up to 24 pages of poetry. Prize of 25 copies of book. $10 reading fee; February 2 deadline. Write for complete guidelines: I.W.I. Chapbook Competition, Illinois State University, I.W.I./Unit

The Avisson Book of Contests and

for Contemporary Literature, Campus Box 4241, Normal, IL 61790.

The LEDGE ANNUAL POETRY CHAPBOOK CONTEST. Write for complete guidelines including deadlines and entry/reading fees. *The Ledge*, c/o Timothy Monaghan, Editor, 64-65 Cooper Avenue, Glendale, NY 11385.

MARYLAND POETRY REVIEW CHAPBOOK CONTEST. For manuscript of 20-24 pages. Is blind competition. Prize of $150 and 50 copies of chapbook. June 1 deadline. *Maryland Poetry Review*, Drawer H, Baltimore, MD 21228.

NAVARRO PUBLICATIONS CHAPBOOK CONTEST. Prize: $50 and 50 copies of finished chapbook. Submit manuscript of 20-40 pages. $10 reading fee; submit between December 17 and July 17. Navarro Publications, P.O. Box 1107, Blythe, CA 92226.

NAVARRO PUBLICATIONS MINI-CHAPBOOK CONTESTS. Prize: $25 and 25 copies of finished chapbook. Submit manuscript of 5-10 poems. $5 reading fee; submit between December 1 and April 1. Navarro Publications, P.O. Box 1107, Blythe, CA 92226.

NEW SPIRIT PRESS CHAPBOOK CONTEST. Write for complete guidelines including deadlines and entry/reading fees. New Spirit Press, 82-34 138 Street, Box 6F, Kew Gardens, NY 11435.

NO ENTRY FEE POETRY CONTEST. Prize: cash awards and publication in anthology. No length limits or restrictions on theme. Poets may enter as many poems or as often as they wish. Send bio/credit sheet. Navarro Publications, P.O. Box 1107, Blythe, California 92226.

NOT JUST ANOTHER POETRY CHAPBOOK COMPETITION: Prize: publication plus 50 copies of finished book. Submit up to 15 pages of poetry. $20 reading fee; February 28 deadline. *Excursus*, P.O. Box 1056, Knickerbocker Station, New York, NY 10002.

PAINTED BRIDE QUARTERLY CHAPBOOK CONTEST. Prize is publication of chapbook. $10 entry fee; July 31 deadline. *Painted Bride Quarterly*, c/o Painted Bride Art Center, 230 Vine Street, Philadelphia, PA 19106.

PALANQUIN PRESS CHAPBOOK CONTEST. Write for complete guidelines including deadlines and entry/reading fees. Send to: Phebe Davidson, Editor, Palanquin/TDM, Department of English, University of South Carolina-Aiken, 171 University Parkway, Aiken, SC 29801.

PAPER BOAT MAGAZINE CHAPBOOK COMPETITION. $200 prize and 50 copies of book. $10 entry fee. June 15 deadline. Paper Boat Press, P.O. Box 2615, Poulsbo, WA 98370.

PAVEMENT SAW CHAPBOOK CONTEST. $500 and 25 copies of published book. Submit manuscript of up to 32 pages. $7 reading fee; December 20 deadline. Pavement Saw Press, 7 James Street, Scotia, NY 12302.

PEARL CHAPBOOK CONTEST. For 20-24 page manuscript of poetry. First prize of $500 plus 50 copies of book. Is blind competition. $10 reading fee; July 1 deadline. *Pearl*, 3030 E. Second Street, Long Beach, CA 90803-1994

PERIVALE PRESS POETRY CHAPBOOK CONTEST. For a 20-page manuscript of poetry. $100 prize plus 60 copies of book. $12 entry fee. Submit only during April or May. Write Perivale Press, 13830 Erwin Street, Van Nuys, CA 91401-2914.

PERMAFROST CHAPBOOK COMPETITION. For a 24-36 page manuscript. $100 prize plus publication. $10 reading fee. March 1 deadline. *Permafrost*, English Department,

Universitiy of Alaska, Fairbanks, AK 99775

PUDDING HOUSE POETRY CHAPBOOK COMPETITION. For poetry on the following themes, topics: social concerns, human services, interpersonal relations, popular culture, justice issues and work drawn from journal writing. The prize: $100 and publication. Submit 10-30 poems. $10 entry fee; June 30 deadline. Pudding House Poetry Chapbook Competition, *Pudding* Magazine, 60 N. Main St., Johnston, OH 43031.

QUENTIN R. HOWARD POETRY PRIZE (see Wind's Annual Poetry Chapbook Competition, this section).

◆RICHARD A. SEFFRON MEMORIAL AWARD. *For poets who are not over 30 years of age.* Prize: 40% of press run. Submit 8-12 pages of poetry; finalists will be asked to send longer manuscript. No entry fee; June 30 deadline. Send for guidelines to: Pygmy Forest Press, P.O. Box 591, Albion, California 95410.

RIVERSTONE CHAPBOOK CONTEST. For a 20-24 page manuscript. $100 cash prize and 50 copies of book.$8 reading fee. June 30 deadline. Riverstone Press, 1184-A MacPherson Drive, West Chester, PA 19380.

RUAH CHAPBOOK COMPETITION. Manuscripts of spiritual poetry up to 24 pages. $10 reading fee. Winner receives 10 copies of *Ruah*. Postmark deadline: March 15. Send to: Editors, *Ruah*, 2401 Ridge Road, Berkeley, CA 94709.

SADDLE MOUNTAIN PRESS CHAPBOOK CONTEST. For manuscript of 12-16 pages of poetry. Prize of publication and 25 copies of chapbook. $9 reading fee; August 15 deadline. Saddle Mountain Press, 1434 6th Street, Astoria, OR 97103.

SARASOTA POETRY THEATRE CHAPBOOK COMPETITION. For 20-24 page manuscript. First prize of $50 plus 25 copies of book;

Prize Competitions *for Poets*

$10 entry fee; August 15 deadline. Sarasota Poetry Theatre, P.O. Box 48955, Sarasota, FL 34230.

SCARS PUBLICATIONS POETRY CHAPBOOK CONTEST. Prize is publication and 25 copies of book. Send manuscript of up to 24 pages. Entry fee $10. Ongoing deadline. Scars Publications, 2543 North Kimball, Chicago IL 60647.

SIDEWALKS CHAPBOOK COMPETITION. For poets with no more than one published book of poetry. Submit 20-25 page manuscript [two copies]. $10 reading fee; February 15 deadline. Sidewalks Chapbook Contest, P.O. Box 321, Champlin, MN 55316.

◆ SLAPERING HOL PRESS CHAPBOOK COMPETITION. *For poets who have not yet published a book or chapbook.* $200 prize and 10 copies of book. Send manuscript of 20-24 pages with acknowledgments page and bio. $10 reading fee. April 15 deadline. Contest, Hudson Valley Writers Center, P.O. Box 366, Tarrytown, NY 10591.

SLIPSTREAM POETRY CHAPBOOK CONTEST. $500 prize and chapbook publiction, plus 50 copies of winning book. Submit manuscript of up to 40 pages. $10 reading fee; December 1 deadline. Chapbook Contest, *Slipstream*, Box 2071, New Market Station, Niagara Falls, NY 14301. OK

SOUNDPOST PRESS POETRY CHAPBOOK COMPETITION. For poetry manuscripts of 24 pages or less. Prize of $100 plus 20 copies of chapbook. $10 entry fee. May 10 deadline. Soundpost Press, 1104 Charles Street, Columbia, MO 65201.

◆ SOUTHWEST POETS' SERIES CHAPBOOK COMPETITION. *Open only to residents of Arizona, New Mexico, Colorado, Nevada, Oklahoma, Texas, Utah, and California.* For poetry manuscript not exceeding 24 pages. First prize of 50 copies plus publication. $10 reading fee; October 31 deadline. Maverick Press, Route 2, Box 4915, Eagle Pass, TX 78852.

SOW'S EAR CHAPBOOK COMPETITION. $500 first prize, $100 second prize, $100 third prize, plus copies of finished book and publication. Submit manuscript of 20-25 pages. $10 reading fee. Submit during March and April only. Chapbook Competition, *Sow's Ear Review*, 19535 Pleasant View Drive, Abingdon, VA 24211-6827.

STILL WATERS PRESS POETRY CHAPBOOK COMPETITION. Write for complete guidelines including deadlines and entry/reading fees. Still Waters Press, 112 W. Duerer Street, Galloway, NJ 08201-9402.

TEARS IN THE FENCE PAMPHLET COMPETITION. Write for complete guidelines including deadlines and entry/reading fees. *Tears in the Fence*, 38 Hod View, Stourpaine, Blandford Forum, Dorset DT11 8TN, England.

TENNESSEE CHAPBOOK CONTEST. For manuscript of poetry or short play, 20-24 pages in length. Prize: publication plus 50 copies of chapbook. $10 reading fee (includes issue of magazine). *Poems & Plays*, Gay Brewer, editor, English Department, Middle Tennessee State University, Murfreesboro, TN 37132.

WHITE EAGLE COFFEE STORE PRESS CHAPBOOK CONTEST. $150 prize plus publication. For manuscript of 20-24 pages. $10 reading fee; March 30 deadline. White Eagle Coffee Store Press, Box 383, Fox River Grove, IL 60021.

WILLIAM AND KINGMAN PAGE CHAPBOOK AWARD. Prize: $500 plus publication and 50 copies of finished chapbook. Submit manuscripts of up to 31 pages, maximum 43 lines per page. Is blind competition. $10 reading fee; November 1 deadline. Send for guidelines to Chapbook Award, Potato Eyes

Foundation, P.O. Box 76, Troy, ME 04987.

WIND'S ANNUAL POETRY CHAPBOOK COMPETITION. (Quentin R. Howard Poetry Prize). For chapbook-length manuscript. Write for complete guidelines including deadlines and entry/reading fees. *Wind* Chapbook Competition, PO Box 24548, Lexington, KY 40524.

SINGLE POEM CONTESTS

Prize Competitions *for Poets*

◆●ALABAMA STATE COUNCIL ON THE ARTS LITERARY FELLOWSHIPS. Including poetry. *For Alabama residents at least two years at time of application.* The prize: $5,000. May 1 deadline for following year. Alabama State Council on the Arts, 201 Monroe St., Montgomery, AL 36130.

ALLEN TATE MEMORIAL POETRY PRIZE. For an unpublished poem of any length. $500 and magazine publication. $2 per poem entry fee; June 30 deadline. Allen Tate Memorial Poetry Prize, Wind Magazine, P.O. Box 24548, Lexington, KY 40524.

ALICE SHERRY MEMORIAL PRIZE. For humorous poetry. The prizes: $25, $15, $10. Submit poem 32 lines maximum. January 15 deadline. Alice Sherry Memorial Prize, The Poetry Society of Virginia, 4712 Old Dominion Dr., Lynchburg, VA 24503.

ALLIGATOR JUNIPER prizes. Includes poetry. $500 prize for best poem. Reading fee $10, for up to five pages of poetry. February 28 deadline. Send for complete guidelines. *Alligator Juniper*, Prescott College, 220 Grove Avenue, Prescott, AZ 86301.

ALLEN GINSBERG POETRY AWARDS. Prizes of $300; $150; $100, and publication in literary magazine. Is blind competition. Submit up to five poems. $12 entry fee; April 1 deadline. Poetry Center, Passaic County Community College, One College Boulevard, Paterson, NJ 07505.

AMELIA MAGAZINE AWARDS (various contests).
—Amelia Encore Award. For previously published poem, 50 lines or less in length. $50 prize; $3 reading fee.
—Amelia Native American Poetry Award, fee $4 each poem. For best previously published poem maximum 50 lines;
—Anna B. Janzen Romantic Poetry Award. For poem to 100 lines in length. $100 prize. $4 reading fee.

49

—Ardis Walker Haiku Award; write for details.
—Ardis Walker Poetry Award. For photo, cartoon/illustration. $50 prize. $3 entry fee;
—Bernice Jennings Poetry Award. For poem up to 100 lines in length. $100 prize; $4 reading fee.
—Charles William Duke Longpoem Award. For longpoem of any length, possible chapbook publication and $150; $10 reading fee;
—Cicada Award. For single poem written in oriental or Eastern form. $100 prize. $4 entry fee.
—Cicada Chapbook Award. For poetry manuscript up to 16 pages in length. Oriental or Eastern forms. $10 entry fee.
—Dak Rambo Gay/Lesbian Poetry Award. For best poem up to 100 lines; $5 reading fee.
—Erin Patrick Raborg Children's Poetry Award. For best poem on theme of children. $3 entry fee.
—Georgie Starbuck Galbraith Light/Humorous Verse Awards; for humorous verse.
—Lester R. Cash Short Poem Awards. For poems 14 lines or less. Various cash prizes. $3 reading fee, each poem;
—The Lucille Sandberg Haiku Awards. For the haiku form.$3 reading fee each poem;
—Marguerette Cummins Broadside Award, $50 prize For best poem up to 500 lines. $5 reading fee.

For the above contests, write for complete guidelines and deadlines to *Amelia* magazine, 329 "E" Street, Bakersfield, CA 93304.

AMERICAN LITERARY REVIEW poetry contest. $500 prize plus publication; additional submissions may be published. Submit up to 3 poems. $10 reading fee; September 15 deadline. *American Literary Review*, University of North Texas, P.O. Box 13827, Denton, TX 76203.

AMERICAN POETS contest. For poetry up to 20 lines in length. $300 grand prize. Write for complete guidelines including deadlines and entry/reading fees. Contact: Poetry Contest, 1737 Enterprise Drive, Troy, MI 48083.

Prize Competitions *for Poets*

AMERICAS REVIEW poetry contest. For "high quality poetry" with "social and political content." Original poetry only; but may be translations. Prizes: four first prizes, $100 each and publication. $8 reading fee covers 3-5 poems; February 28 deadline. Contest, *Americas Review*, P.O. Box 7681, Berkeley, CA 94707.

AMETHYST REVIEW WRITING CONTEST. Write for complete guidelines including deadlines and entry/reading fees. *The Amethyst Review*, 23 Riverside Ave., Truro, Nova Scotia, B2N 4G2, Canada.

◆AMY AWARD. *Open to women 30 years of age or younger who are residents of New York City or Long Island.* For lyric poems, not exceeding 50 lines each. Send 3 poems with short biographical statement. Prize: Scheduled reading and honorarium. Amy Award, Guild Hall, 158 Main Street, Easthampton, NY 11937.

ANN STANFORD POETRY PRIZE. Prizes of $750, $250, $100. Write for complete guidelines including deadlines and entry/reading fees: The Southern California Anthology, c/o University of Southern California, WPH 404, Los Angeles, CA 90089.

ANNA DAVIDSON ROSENBERG AWARD FOR POEMS ON THE JEWISH EXPERIENCE. Write for complete guidelines including deadlines and entry/reading fees. Send to: Poetry Award, Judah Magnes Museum, 2911 Russell Street, Berkeley, CA 94705.

◆ANTIETAM REVIEW LITERARY AWARDS. $50 prize plus publication. Submit up to 5 poems; $3 reading fee per poem. Individual poems should not exceed 30 lines in length. *Open only to residents or natives of the following states: Maryland, Virginia, West Virginia, Pennsylvania, Delaware, or the District of Columbia.* Write to: *Antietam Review*, 7 West Franklin Street, Hagerstown, MD 21740.

ARIZONA AUTHORS ASSOCIATION NATIONAL LITERARY CONTEST. Including poetry. Is blind competition. The prizes: $125;$75; $40; $10, and publication in the *Arizona Literary Magazine*. *Length:* 42 line maxiumum. $5 entry fee each poem; July 29 postmark deadline. Arizona Authors Association, National Literary Contest, 3509 E. Shea Blvd., #117, Phoenix, AZ 85028-3339.

ARVON INTERNATIONAL POETRY COMPETITION. Sponsored every odd-numbered year; next competition in 1997. Prizes of 5,000 British pounds; 500 British pounds; 250 British pounds; and publication in anthology. Write for current entry fee and guidelines. Entry form required. Arvon International Poetry Competition, Arvon Foundation, Kilnhurst, Kilnhurst Road, Todmorden, Lancashire OL14 6AX, England.

ART IN THE AIR POETRY CONTEST. $100 first prize, for a poem up to 75 lines. Is thematic contest; write for current themes. Deadline, October 31. *Inventing the Invisible*, 3128 Walton Boulevard, Suite 186, Rochester Hills, MI 48309.

ARTISTS EMBASSY INTERNATIONAL DANCING POETRY CONTEST. Cash prizes, cretificates awarded. Three Grand Prizes of presentation of poems as dance performance with choreography, costumes, etc., with broadcast on cable television. Submit poems of up to 40 lines. Entry fee $5 for one poem, $10 for up to three poems; June 1 deadline. Write for guidelines; Contest Chair, 704 Brigham Ave., Santa Rosa, CA 95404.

ASCHER MONTANDON AWARD IN POETRY. For three unpublished poems. The prize: publication in *Hyper Age* literary magazine. *Hyper Age*, Ascher Montandon Award in Poetry, 1388 Haight St., #13, San Francisco, CA 94117.

ASTREA LESBIAN WRITERS FUND. Including poetry, for lesbians. The prize: $10,000 grant. Write for complete guidelines

Prize Competitions *for Poets*

including deadlines and entry/reading fees. Astrea National Lesbian Action Foundation, Lesbian Writers Fund, 116 East 16 St, 7th Flr, New York NY 10003.

BARBARA MANDINGO KELLY PEACE POETRY AWARDS. For a poem showing "aspects of peace and the human spirit." $1,000 in total prizes, plus publication. Is blind competition. Has Youth category; open categories. Send up to three poems, with a 40 line maximum. Reading fee (adults) $5; youth categories, free; June 30 deadline. Guidelines: NAPF Poetry Awards, 1187 Coart Village Road, Suite 123, Santa Barbara, CA 93108.

BAXTER HATHAWAY PRIZE, Write for complete guidelines including deadlines and entry/reading fees. *Epoch*, Cornell University, 251 Goldwin Smith Ithaca, NY 14853-3201 F,P

BAY AREA POETS COALITION CONTEST. Write for complete guidelines including deadlines and entry/reading fees. Mark States, BAPC Contest 16, PO Box 11435, Berkeley, CA 94712-2435.

BERNARD F. CONNERS PRIZE FOR POETRY. Prize: $1,000. For a poem, minimum length 200 lines, published annually in the *Paris Review*. All submissions as submissions to the Review. No entry fee; continuing deadline. The *Paris Review*, 541 East 7 Street, New York, NY 10021.

BERNICE SLOTE AWARD. Includes poetry. For the best poem published in an issue of *Prairie Schooner* literary magazine. The prize: $500. Submit only as submission to the literary magazine. Bernice Slote Award, *Prairie Schooner*, University of Nebraska, 201 Andrews, Lincoln, NE 68588-0334.

◆BILLEE MURRAY DENNY POETRY CONTEST. *For poets who have not previously published a book-length work of poetry.* Prizes of $1,000, $500, $250. Submit 1-3 original, unpublished poems; individual poems must not exceed 100 lines in length. Entry fee: $10 per poem; deadline May 31 postmark. Send for guidelines. Billee Murray Denny Poetry Contest, c/o Janet Overton, Lincoln College, 300 Kookuk Street, Lincoln, IL 62656.

BLACK WARRIOR REVIEW prizes. Includes poetry. Prize: $500. For the best poem published in each of two issues (spring and fall) of the Review. Submit only as a submission to the Review. Deadlines: July 15 and January 15. *The Black Warrior Review.* University of Alabama, P0 Box 862936 Tuscaloosa, AL 35486.

BLUE UNICORN poetry contest. First prize is $100 and publication, other cash prizes and publication. Postmark deadline: March 1. Hal Bosworth, Contest Chair, *Blue Unicorn*, 921 Ensenada Avenue, Berkeley, CA 94707.

BORDERLANDS POETRY CONTEST. Submit ten or more pages of poetry. $500 cash prize. $10 entry fee. Submit between March 1 and May 1. *Borderlands Magazine*, Box 49818, Austin, TX 78765.

BRIAR CLIFF REVIEW POETRY COMPETITION. $150 prize, publication. Submit up to three poems. $10 entry fee. *Briar Cliff Review* Competition, Briar Cliff College, 3303 Rebecca Street, Sioux City, IA 51104.

THE BRIDGE POETRY CONTEST. For poem to 75 lines. Prizes of $75, $50, and publication. $3 per poem entry fee; February 25 deadline. No guidelines. Send poems to "Contest," 14050 Vernon St., Oak Park, MI 48237.

◆●THE BRIO [BRONX RECOGNIZES ITS OWN] FELLOWSHIPS offer $1,500 to Bronx artists in various disciplines including fiction, poetry, playwriting/screenwriting, and nonfiction literature. The Council also offers technical assistance to Bronx writers and is in the process of developing the Bronx Writers Center, a haven for writers in the Bronx. Write for complete guidelines and application forms. Deadline: February 15. Bronx Council on the Arts, 1738 Hone Avenue, Bronx, NY 10461.

BRODIE HERNDON MEMORIAL. For poems about the sea. Submit poems, 48 lines maximum. January 15 deadline. Brodie Herndon Memorial, The Poetry Society of Virginia, 6042 Newport Crescent, Norfolk, VA 23505.

BUFFALO BONES POETRY CONTEST. 1st Prize $150; second, $75; third $50. For poems up to 40 lines. Reading fee, $5 for three poems; $10 for six. November 1 deadline. Send to: Evergreen Poets & Writers, P.O. Box 714, Evergreen, CO 80437.

BYRON ROBERTS REESE INTERNATIONAL POETRY AWARDS. The prizes: six $450 awards. January 31 deadline. Write for current guidelines. Byron Roberts Reese International Poetry Awards, Georgia State Poetry Society, 4331 Chimney Court, Roswell, GA 30075.

CALIFORNIA STATE POETRY SOCIETY CONTEST. Open to all poets in the U.S. Prizes of $100, $70, $30, $10. Submit poems of up to 40 lines. $3 reading fee; submit between March 1 and May 31. Write for guidelines. Contest Chair: 2780 Hillcrest Drive, La Verne, CA 91750.

◆CAPRICON POETRY AWARD. *Given to a poet "of excellence" who is over forty years of age.* $1,000 prize for poet's reading at The Writer's Voice. $15 reading fee; December 31 deadline. Send for guidelines and entry form. The Writer's Voice of the West Side YMCA, 5 West 63rd Street, New York, NY 10023.

CARL CHERRY CENTER FOR THE ARTS poetry contest. Solicits "verse from the unconscious mind." Cash awards, books, certificates of merit. Limited to three poems of not more than

24 lines per poem. Entry fee: $7 per poem. Deadline: March 24. Carl Cherry Center for the Arts, P.O. Box 863, Carmel, CA 93921.

CARL SANDBURG LITERARY ARTS AWARDS. Write for complete guidelines including deadlines and entry/reading fees. Friends of the Chicago Public Library, 400 South State St., 9S-7 Chicago, IL 60605

◆●CAVE CANEM WORKSHOP FOR AFRICAN AMERICAN POETS. Prize: free attendance at workshop. Awarded to up to 36 participants, based on excellence and number of manuscripts received. At the Alphonsus Retreat Center, Hudson River, 90 miles north of New York City. Submit 6-8 poems. February 28 deadline. Toi Derricotte, Cave Canem, University of Pittsburgh, Department of English, 526 CL, Pittsburgh, PA 15260-0001.

◆CECIL HEMLEY MEMORIAL AWARD. *Open to Poetry Society of America members only.* For a lyric poem on a philosophical theme, 100 lines maximum. The prize: $300. December 22 deadline. Cecil Hemley Memorial Award, Poetry Society of America, 15 Gramercy Park, New York, NY 10003.

CHAD WALSH POETRY AWARD. For a poem or group of poems published in the *Beloit Poetry Journal* the previous year. The prize: $4,000. Submit poetry to the *Beloit Poetry Journal* for possible publication during current year for following year's award. *The Beloit Poetry Journal,* The Chad Walsh Poetry Award, RFD 2, Box 154, Ellsworth, ME 04065.

CHARLES B. WOOD AWARD FOR DISTINGUISHED WRITING. $500 for the best poem or short story by "an emerging writer" published during the year in the *Carolina Quarterly.* Submissions only as a submission to the magazine. Write: The Editors, *Carolina Quarterly,* 510 Greenlaw Hall CB #3520, University of North Carolina, Chapel Hill, NC 27599

Prize Competitions *for Poets*

◆CHARLES JOHNSON AWARDS. Includes poetry. *Open only to "ethnic minority" college students or writers whose work "explores the experience / identity of a minority or marginalized culture."* $500 prize. Submit 3-5 poems, total length of not more than six pages. No entry fee listed; inquire for deadlines. Charles Johnson Awards, Southern Illinois University—Carbondale, Department of English, Carbondale, IL 62901.

CHATTAHOOCHIE REVIEW POETRY CONTEST. For individual poems up to 60 lines. Awards of $100 and publication. Entry fee $10.00 for up to three poems, $2.00 each additional poem. Send for guidelines to Contest, *The Chattahoochie Review,* Dekalb College, 2101 Womack Road, Dunwoody, GA 30338.

CHELSEA AWARD COMPETITION. Includes poetry. Prize: $750 plus publication in magazine. For the best group of 4-6 poems, less than 500 lines total. $10 reading fee includes subscription to magazine; December 15 deadline. Write for complete guidelines to *Chelsea,* P.O. Box 1040, York Beach, ME 03910.

CHIRON REVIEW POETRY CONTEST. Write for complete guidelines including deadlines and entry/reading fees. *Chiron Review* Poetry Contest, Jane Hathaway, Contest Chairperson, 522 E. South Ave., St. John, KS 67576.

CLARK COLLEGE POETRY CONTEST. For poem of 50 lines or less. Is blind competition. Prizes of $200, $150, $100, and publication. $3 entry fee, each poem; February 10 deadline. For guidelines, write: Clark College Poetry Contest, 1800 E. McLoughlin Blvd., Vancouver, WA 98663.

COLUMBIA JOURNAL OF LITERATURE AND ART poetry competition. $250 cash prize and possible publication in magazine. Submit up to 10 pages of poetry. $7 reading fee. February 14 deadline.

Competition, *Columbia Journal*, Columbia University, 415 Dodge Hall, New York, NY 10027.

COUNCIL ON NATIONAL LITERATURES POETRY AWARD. For poem "expressing multicultural diversity" in positive manner and/or "reflecting national history." $100 prize and publication. $3 reading fee; August 31 deadline. CNL Poetry Award, Potpourri Publications, Box 8278, Prairie Village, KS 66208.

CRAB CREEK REVIEW POETRY CONTEST. December 15 deadline. Send for complete guidelines. Poetry Contest, *Crab Creek Review*, 4462 Whitman Avenue North, Seattle, WA 98103.

CREAM CITY REVIEW POETRY CONTEST. $100 first place prize plus magazine publication. Submit 3-5 poems, not to exceed 100 lines per poem. Entry fee $5. June 30 deadline. *The Cream City Review*, Department of English, University of Wisconsin at Milwaukee, P.O. Box 413, Milwaukee, WI 53201.

DANCING WORDS PRESS POETRY CONTEST. For a single unpublished poem. $500 prize. $2 entry fee per poem; December 31 deadline. Write Dancing Words Poetry Contest, Dancing Words Press, 449 Ninth St., Gretna, LA 70053.

DANIEL VAROUJAN PRIZE. For an original poem that best "embodies the spirit" of the Armenian poet Daniel Varoujan. $500 prize. Submit one unpublished poem in duplicate. $3 entry fee; this fee is waived for membership in the New England Poetry Club. April 24 deadline. Daniel Varoujan Prize, New England Poetry Club, 2 Farrar Street, Cambridge, MA 02138.

DAVID ROSS MEMORIAL COMPETITION. Includes poetry. Prizes of $250, $150, $100; publication in anthology. April 30 deadline. *The Scriveners*, P.O. Box 20550, Wichita, KS 67208.

DEAR DIARY CONTEST. Write for complete guidelines including

deadlines and entry/reading fees. Log Cabin Dear Diary Contest, PO Box 1536, Allentown, PA 18105.

DEDICATED POETS COMPETITION. For individual poems up to 50 lines. Cash prizes of $250, $100, $50, honorable mentions. Entry fee $10, covers up to 10 poems. February 29 deadline. Treasure House Publishing, 1106 Oak Hill Avenue, No. 3A, Hagerstown, MD 21742.

DEEP SOUTH WRITERS CONFERENCE poetry contest. $650 in poetry awards, in connection with writer's conference. Is blind competition Submit 1-3 poems. $10 reading fee; July 15 deadline. Send for guidelines to: Contest Coordinator, Deep South Writers Conference, c/o Department of English, USL Box 44691, University of Southwestern Louisiana, Lafayette, LA 70504.

◆DISCOVERY/THE NATION JOAN LEIMAN JACOBSON POETRY PRIZES. *For a selection of poems by an unpublished poet.* The prize: $300, publication and reading at the Poetry Center. Is blind competition. Submit a ten-page manuscript, total lines not exceeding 500. Send for complete guidelines and current deadline: *Discovery*/The Nation Joan Leiman Jacobson Poetry Prizes, The Unterburg Poetry Center, 92 St. YM-YWCA, 1395 Lexington Ave., New York, NY 10128.

DISHEARTENING SOULS REVIEW POETRY CONTEST. Write for complete guidelines including deadlines and entry/reading fees. *Disheartening Souls Review,* P.O. Box 426, Mantua, OH 44255.

DOG WRITERS' ASSOCIATION OF AMERICA WRITING COMPETITION. Includes poetry. For writing on all aspects of care, training, life with a dog. The prizes: cash, honor plaques, certificates. October 1 deadline. Dog Writers' Association of America Writing Competition, 5714 Folsom Blvd., #117, Sacramento, CA 95852.

DOROTHY DANIELS HONORARY WRITING AWARD COMPETITION. The Simi Valley Branch of the National League of American Pen Women, Inc. Write for complete guidelines including deadlines and entry/reading fees. Mail to: NLAPW-SVB Entries, PO Box 1485, Simi Valley, CA 93062.???

EDWARD STANLEY AWARD. For the year's best poem or group of poems published in *Prairie Schooner* literary magazine. The prize: $500. Edward Stanley Award, *Prairie Schooner*, University of Nebraska, 201 Andrews, Lincoln, NE 68588.

THE EIGHTH MOUNTAIN POETRY COMPETITION. Awarded in even-numbered years. The prize: $1,000. Write for complete guidelines including deadlines and entry/reading fees. Poetry Prize, The Eighth Mountain Press, 624 SE 29th Ave., Portland, OR 97214-3026.

ELIZABETH MATCHETT STOVER MEMORIAL AWARD. Write for complete guidelines including deadlines and entry/reading fees. *Southwest Review*, 307 Fondren Library West, Box 374, Southern Methodist Univ., Dallas, TX 75275.

ELMER HOLMES BOBST AWARDS. Write for complete guidelines including deadlines and entry/reading fees. New York University Press, Bobst Library, 70 Washington Square S., 2nd Fl., New York, NY 10012-1091

◆EMILY DICKINSON AWARD. For Poetry Society of America members only. For a poem inspired by Emily Dickinson, but not necessarily written in her style. The prize: $100. Submit manuscript of 30 lines maximum. October 1-December 31 submission dates. Emily Dickinson Award, Poetry Society of America, 15 Gramercy Park, New York, NY 10003.

EMILY DICKINSON POETRY AWARD. $500 prize and publication in anthology. Unpublished poems only. Submit up to three poems, total pages six or less, with a brief biographical note.

Prize Competitions *for Poets*

$9 reading fee. Deadline: July 31 postmark. Emily Dickinson Award in Poetry, Universities West Press, P.O. Box 697, Williams, AZ 86046.

EMILY CLARK BALCH AWARDS, Write for complete guidelines including deadlines and entry/reading fees. *Virginia Quarterly Review,* One West Range, Charlottesville, VA 22903.

EVE OF ST. AGNES AWARD IN POETRY. $1,000 prize and publication in magazine. Is blind competition. Reading fee $3 per poem; January 15 deadline. Write for guidelines: *Negative Capability,* 62 Ridgelawn Drive East, Mobile, AL 36608.

EXCURSUS LITERARY ARTS JOURNAL POETRY CONTEST. $200 cash prize plus publication in magazine. 250 line maximum. Entry fee $5 for up to 5 poems. June 30 deadline. *Excursus* Magazine, P.O. Box 1056, Knickerbocker Station, New York, NY 10002.

EXPLORATIONS LITERARY CONTEST. $500 prize and publication in *Explorations* literary magazine. Submit manuscript of up to five poems, poem limit 60 lines each. Entry fee $5 first two poems, $2 each additional. March 21 postmark deadline. University of Alaska Southeast, *Explorations* Literary Contest, 11120 Glacier Highway, Juneau, AK 99801.

EYSTER PRIZE-NEW DELTA REVIEW. Includes poetry. For the best work submitted and published in each issue of *New Delta Review.* The prize: cash. March 15 and October 15 closing dates for the spring/summer and fall/winter issues respectively. Eyster Prize-*New Delta Review,* Louisiana State University, English Dept., Baton Rouge, LA 70803-5001.

FELIX POLLAK POETRY AWARD. Write for complete guidelines including deadlines and entry/reading fees. *The Madison Review,.* Department of English, University of Wisconsin, 600 North Park St., Madison, WI 53706.

◆●FELLOWS OF THE WINSONSIN INSTITUTE FOR CREATIVE WRITING. Including poets. The prize: $20,000 and an academic year in residence at the University of Wisconsin Institute for Creative Writing. One reading from works in progress and the teaching of one introductory workshop in creative writing each semester. *For writers who have completed an MFA or an equivalent creative writing degree and have not published a book.* Submit 10 pages of poetry. University of Wisconsin, Fellows of the Wisconsin Institute for Creative Writing, Department of English, 600 N. Park St., Madison, WI 53706.

◆●FINE ARTS WORK CENTER IN PROVINCETOWN SENIOR FELLOWSHIP Program. *For poets over 50 years of age* who have won earlier recognition and are now re-emerging with new work. The prize: six $1,500 honorarium each including an apartment for one month at the Fine Arts Work Center. July 1 deradline. Provincetown, Massachusetts. May 1 deadline. 24 Pearl Street, Provincetown, MA 02657.

FIRMAN HOUGHTON PRIZE. For lyric poem. The prize: $250. Submit in duplicate. $3 entry fee. May 30 deadline. Firman Houghton Prize, New England Poetry Club, 2 Farrar St., Cambridge, MA 02138.

FIVE POINTS POETRY CONTEST. $500 and publication for a group of three to five poems. Submit as many as five poems. $10 reading fee; November 15 deadline. Five Points Poetry Contest, Georgia State University, Department of English, University Plaza, Atlanta, GA 30303-3083.

THE FLORIDA REVIEW EDITOR'S AWARDS IN POETRY. $500 prize and publication. Submit 3-5 poems, maximum 25 lines each. $10 reading fee (includes subscription to magazine); March 15 deadline. Editors' Awards in Poetry, *The Florida Review*, Department of English, University of Central Florida, Orlando, FL 32816.

Prize Competitions *for Poets*

FLORIDA INTERNATIONAL UNIVERSITY POETRY COMPETITION. For a poem published within the current or previous year. The prize: $2,000 to be split between the literary magazine as publisher and the author. Poets should contact their magazine editor for possible submission. Submit 2 copies of the magazine containing the poem. Limit of one poem/poet per magazine publisher. No entry fee; March 15 deadline. Poetry Competition, Florida International University, University Park and North Miami Campuses, Miami, FL 33199.

FLYWAY WRITING AWARDS. Includes poetry. Prize of $100 plus publication in magazine. $10 reading fee covers up to 3 poems. March 1 deadline. Flyway Writing Awards, English Department, 203 Ross Hall, Iowa State University, Ames, Iowa 50011.

FOSTER CITY WRITERS CONTEST. Includes poetry. The prize: $300. Submit poetry manuscript, 2-page limit double spaced. April 2-August 31 submission dates. Foster City Writers Contest, Foster City Arts & Cultural Committee, 650 Shell Blvd., Foster City, CA 94404.

◆●FRANCES SHAW FELLOWSHIP. *For a woman poet who began writing seriously over the age of 55.* The prize: a two-month residency in the summer or the fall, including living quarters, private living and work space, meals, and transportation to and from Ragdale. Submit 10 poems. February 1 deadline. Ragdale Foundation, Frances Shaw Fellowship, 1260 N. Green Bay Rd, Lake Forest, IL 60045.

◆●FULBRIGHT SCHOLAR AWARDS. Including poetry and poetry translations. The prize: grants for research and lecturing abroad from 2 months to an academic year, travel and living allowances included. Assignment to more than 100 countries, some multi-country awards available. For professionals, writers, independent scholars outside the academic arena.

63

Must have a Ph.D or equivalent status, teaching experience, U.S. citizenship, proficiency in foreign language helps, but not required. August 1 deadline. Council for International Exchange of Scholars, 3007 Tilden St. NW, #5M, Washington DC 20008-3009.

A GATHERING OF THE TRIBES POETRY CONTEST. $500 first prize. Reading fee, $10. Deadline April 1. Send a maximum three poems, each 20 lines or less. A Gathering of the Tribes, Inc., P.O. Box 20693, Tompkins Square Station, New York, NY 10009.

GEORGETOWN REVIEW poetry contest. $150 prize plus publication in magazine. August 1 deadline. Send for guidelines to *Georgetown Review*, 400 East College Street, Georgetown, KY 40324.

GEORGIA STATE UNIVERSITY REVIEW WRITING CONTESTS . Includes poetry. $800 prize and publication in magazine. Submit up to three poems, no length limit; $10 entry fee. April 30 deadline. *Georgia State University Review*, Writing Contests, Georgia State University, Atlanta GA 30303.

GEORGE BOGIN MEMORIAL AWARD. $500 prize. For a group of 4-5 poems, which "uses language in an original way" and "takes a stand against oppression in any of its forms." $5 entry fee applies only to non-members of Poetry Society of America; December 22 deadline. Write for guidelines and entry form to Poetry Society of America, 15 Gramercy Park, New York, NY 10003

GRAFFITI RAG POETRY AWARD. $500 prize plus publication in magazine. Submit 3-5 unpublished poems. $10 reading fee. April 30 deadline. *Graffiti Rag*, 5647 Oakman Blvd., Dearborn, MI 48126.

GREEN RIVER WRITERS CONTESTS. (various contests in poetry and fiction) $1200 in prizes. October 31 deadline. Write for complete guidelines including deadlines and entry/reading fees. Categories: 1. Green River Grande 2. One-Eyed Fish Prize 3. Hub City Prize 4. Woodrow Hale Memorial Prize 5. Pennington Prize 6. Miller Prize. Contest Chair, 1043 Thornfield Lane, Cincinnati, OH 45224.

GREENSBORO REVIEW LITERARY AWARDS. $250 prize; all entries considered for magazine publication. September 15 deadline. Write for complete guidelines. *The Greensboro Review*, c/o English Department, University of North Carolina at Greensboro, Greensboro, NC 27412.

◆GROLIER POETRY PRIZE. *For poets who have not yet published a book.* Two winners selected; $150 and publication in magazine for each winner. $6 entry fee. Ongoing deadline. Grolier Poetry Prize, 6 Plympton Street, Cambridge, MA 02138.

GUY OWEN POETRY PRIZE. $500 and magazine publication. Submit 3-5 poems only. $8 entry fee. Deadline: submit only during month of April. Guy Owen Poetry Prize, *Southern Poetry Review*, Advancement Studies Department, Central Piedmont Community College, Charlotte, NC 28235.

HACKNEY LITERARY AWARDS. Includes poetry. In connection with the annual Writing Today Writers Conference. $2,000 in total prizes. Entry form and entry fee required. December 31 deadline. For submission guidelines write Hackney Literary Awards, Birmingham Southern College, Box 549003, Birmingham, AL 35254.

HALF TONES TO JUBILEE POETRY CONTEST. The prizes: $300, $200, $100. $2 per poem entry fee; May 15 deadline. Poetry Contest, Half Tones to Jubilee, English Dept., Pensacola Junior College, 1,000 College Blvd., Pensacola, FL 32504.

HARP-STRINGS ANNUAL CONTESTS. Write for complete guidelines including deadlines and entry/reading fees. Harp-Strings, 310 S. Adams St., Beverly Hills, FL 33464.

HAZEL HALL AWARD FOR POETRY. Write for complete guidelines including deadlines and entry/reading fees. Oregon Institute of Literary Arts , PO Box 10608 , Portland, OR 97210.

HEINOUS PAYNE AWARD. For an outstanding submission in either poetry, fiction, non-fiction, or artwork. Prizes of $300 and $200. $15 reading fee; July 1 deadline. *Burning Car* Magazine, P.O. Box 26692, San Francisco, CA 94126.

HIDDEN RIVER WRITING COMPETITION . Includes poetry. For the best group of three to six poems. Publication in magazine. Entry fee of $15 includes copy of the awards issue. February 15 deadline. *Hidden River* magazine, P.O. Box 2050, Bala Cynwyd, PA 19004.

HOUYHNHNM LITERARY CONTEST. Write for complete guidelines including deadlines and entry/reading fees. Houyhnhnm Literary Contest, The Stable Companion, PO Box 6485, Lafayette, IN 47903.

HOWARD NEMEROV SONNET AWARD. For the sonnet form. $1,000 prize. Winning poem and finalists will be published in *The Formalist* literary magazine. $3 entry fee per poem; June 16 deadline. Howard Nemerov Sonnet Award, T*he Formalist*, 320 Hunter Drive, Evansville, Indiana 47711.

I.E. MAGAZINE CONTEST. Includes poetry. For free or traditional verse, single poem. Prizes of $25, $15, $10 and publication in anthology. Reading fee $2 for one poem; $5 for three poems. January 31 deadline. *IE Magazine*, P.O. Box 73403, Houston, TX 77273.

◆●INDIANA ARTS COMMISSION MASTER FELLOWSHIPS IN

LITERATURE. Biennial, even years. Including poetry. For poets at least 18 years of age and one year or more residency in the state. The prize: $5,000. Indiana Arts Commission, 402 W. Washington St., Room 072, Indianapolis, IN 46204-2741.

INTERNATIONAL IMITATION HEMINGWAY COMPETITION. Includes poetry. The prize: trip for two, to Harry's Bar and American Grill, Florence, Italy. February 1 deadline. International Imitation Hemingway Competition. PEN American Center W., 672 Lafayette Park Pl., #41, Los Angeles, CA 90057.

INTERNATIONAL NARRATIVE CONTEST. For a narrative poem. The prize: cash. Write for complete guidelines including deadlines and entry/reading fees. International Narrative Contest, Poets & Patrons, Inc., 2820 W. Birchwood Ave., Chicago IL 60645.

INTERNATIONAL POETRY COMPETITION. $1,000, $500, $250 prizes plus magazine publication. Entry fee $5 first poem, $2 each additional poem. March 31 deadline. International Poetry Competition, *Atlanta Review,* P.O. Box 8248, Atlanta, GA 30306.

INTERNATIONAL QUARTERLY CROSSING BOIUNDARIES WRITING AWARD. Includes poetry. For a single poem, no length limit. $500 prize and publication. Submit up to five poems. $10 reading fee; February 1 deadline. Guidelines: Creative Boundaries Awards, *International Quarterly,* P.O. Box 10521, Tallahassee, FL 32303.

IOWA WOMAN annual writing contest. Write for complete guidelines including deadlines and entry/reading fees. Iowa Woman Contest, PO Box 680, Iowa City, IA 52244-0680.

ITALO CALVINO WRITING CONTEST. For poetry inspired by Calvino, in the style of Calvino, or related to Calvino's themes. No translations. The prize: $500 and publication in *Writing on the Edge* literary magazine. Submit 15 pages of original poetry maximum. February 1 deadline. *Writing on the Edge*, Italo Calvino Writing Contest, Campus Writing Center, University of California, Davis, CA 95616.

J. FRANKLIN DEW AWARD. Series of 3-4 haiku, single theme. The prizes: $50, $30, $20. January 15 deadline. Write for complete guidelines including entry/reading fees. J. Franklin Dew Award, The Poetry Society of Virginia, 4712 Old Dominion Drive, Lynchburg, VA 24503.

JACK KEROUAC LITERARY PRIZE. For poetry on themes as expressed in the works of Jack Kerouac. Submit up to 15 pages of poetry. $500 first prize. July 1 deadline. Contact the Jack Kerouac Literary Prize, Lowell Historic Preservation Commission, 222 Merrimac Street, Suite 310, Lowell, MA 01852.

THE JEROME J. SHESTACK POETRY PRIZES. Awarded for the "Three best groups" of poems published each year in *The American PoetryReview*. Submit only as a submission to the Review. No deadlin e; no entry fee. *American Poetry Review*, 1721 Walnut Street, Philadelphia, PA 19103.

THE JESSICA NOBEL MAXWELL MEMORIAL PRIZE. Prize of $2,000. Presented for the best poems published each year in *The American Poetry Review*. Submit only as a submission to the Review. No deadline; no entry fee. *American Poetry Review*, 1721 Walnut Street, Philadelphia, PA 19103.

◆JOHN CIARDI LIFETIME ACHIEVEMENT AWARD IN POETRY. *For poets who have published at least one book of poetry, excluding chapbooks.* The prize: $1,000 and publication in *Italiana Americana* literary magazine. Submit 3 copies of one poem, any length. March 1 deadline. *Italian Americana*, John Ciardi Lifetime Achievement Award in Poetry. University of Rhode Island, College of Continuing Education, 80

Prize Competitions *for Poets*

Washington St., Providence, RI 02903.

JOHN KAY IODICE MEMORIAL AWARD. for the best poem on the theme of Caritas. Maximum of 40 lines, maximum of 5 entries, entry fee: $6 for first poem, $3 for each additional poem. Postmark deadline: March 1. Hal Bosworth, Contest Chair, 921 Ensenada Avenue, Berkeley, CA 94707.

●KANSAS NEWMAN COLLEGE MILTON CENTER POST-GRADUATE FELLOWSHIPS. Including poets. For writers with a Christian commitment to complete their first book-length manuscript. The prize: fellowships at the Milton Center for Writers, Kansas Newman College. Submit a proposal and 10 poems of any length. $15 entry fee; January 31 deadline. Kansas Newman College, Milton Center Post-Graduate Fellowships, 3100 McCormick Avenue, Witchita, KS 67213.

KARAMU CONTEST. Including poetry. Published and unpublished entries welcome. The prize: publication in *Karamu* literary magazine. $5 entry fee; April 1 deadline. *Karamu*, Department of English, Eastern Illinois University, Charleston, IL 61920.

KAY SNOW LITERARY CONTEST. The prizes: $200, $100, $50. Including poetry. Mid-May deadline. Kay Snow Literary Contest, Williamette Writers, 9045 SW Barbour Blvd, #5A, Portland, OR 97219.

KUDZU POETRY CONTEST. Write for complete guidelines including deadlines and entry/reading fees: The Editors, Kudzu Poetry Contest, TDM Press, USC-Aaiken, 171 University Parkway, Aiken, SC 29801.

THE LEDGE POETRY AWARDS. For original unpublished poem. Prizes of $500, $200, $100 and magazine publication. Reading fee of $8, first three poems; $2 each additional (includes one issue of magazine); April 30 postmark deadline.

The Ledge Magazine, Poetry Awards, 78-08 83rd Street, Glendale, NY 11385.

◆ LESBIAN WRITERS FUND AWARDS. Several grant awards of $10,000 each, for an "emerging Lesbian writer" with at least some publication credits in magazine, anthology, or book form. Write for complete guidelines including deadlines and entry/reading fees: Astraea National Lesbian Action Foundation, 666 Broadway, Sutie 520, New York, NY 10012.

TENNESSEE WRITERS ALLIANCE LITERARY AWARDS. Write for complete guidelines including deadlines and entry/reading fees: Literary Awards, PO Box 120396, Nashville, TN 37212

LIVE POETS SOCIETY poetry contest. $300 in prizes plus publication in anthology. Send one or more manuscripts of three poems each. $5 reading fee for each 3-poem manuscript; December 31 deadline. The Live Poets Society, 117 Fitch Road, Washington, ME 04574.

LOCAL 7's ANNUAL NATIONAL POETRY COMPETITION. The prizes: $200, $100, $50. July 1-September 30 submission dates. Local 7's Annual National Poetry Competition, Santa Cruz/Monterey Local 7 National Writers Union, Box 2409, Aptos, CA 95001.

◆LOFT-MCKNIGHT WRITERS AWARD. Including poetry. *For Minnesota residents only.* The prizes: two prizes of $10,500, eight of $7,500. November 29 deadline. Loft-McKnight Writers Award, The Loft, Pratt Community Center, 66 Malcom Ave. SE, Minneapolis, MN 55414.

◆●THE LOFT-MENTOR SERIES. Including poetry. *For Minnesota residents only.* The prize: $400 and study briefly with four nationally known mentor-writers throughout the year. Mid-May deadline. The Loft-Mentor Series, The Loft, Pratt

Community Center, 66 Malcolm Ave. SE, Minneapolis, MN 55414.

LOUDEST LAF! LAUREL. Write for complete guidelines including deadlines and entry/reading fees. Scher Maihem Publishing, P.O. Box 313, Avilla, IN 46710.

LOUISIANA LITERATURE PRIZE FOR POETRY. The prize: $400 and publication in *Louisiana Literature*. February 15 deadline. Send for complete guidelines to: Louisiana Literature Prize for Poetry, Southeastern Louisiana University, Box 792, Hammond, LA 70402.

THE LOVE AFFAIR LITERARY CONTEST . Includes poetry. Anyone may submit, but entrants with knowledge of Georgia/Southern themes are given priority. Is blind contest. Send up to two double-spaced pages of poetry. $7 reading fee; February 14 deadline. Send for full guidelines: Love Affair Literary Contest, The Arts Experiment Station, ABAC 45, 2802 Moore Highway, Tifton, GA 31894.

LULLWATER PRIZE FOR POETRY. Prize: $500 and magazine publication. Submit up to five poems. $8 reading fee; March 2 deadline. *Lullwater Review*, Box 22036, Emory University, Atlanta, GA 30322.

LYNDA HULL MEMORIAL POETRY AWARD. $500 for the best short story and the best poem to appear in *Crazyhorse* during the calendar year. *Crazyhorse*, University of Arkansas at Little Rock, English Department, 2801 South University, Little Rock, AR 72204-1099.

◆LYRIC POETRY AWARD. *For a lyric poem written by a member of the Poetry Society of America.* $500 prize. Poems must be 50 lines or less in length. December 22 deadline. Write for complete guidelines to Lyric Poetry Award, Poetry Society of America, 15 Gramercy Park, New York, NY 10003.

THE LYRIC POETRY PRIZES. (QUARTERLY) For poems published in *The Lyric* literary magazine. The prizes: $800 total. Submit poetry to magazine editors. Quarterly issue deadlines. *The Lyric*, 307 Dunton St. SW, Blacksburg, VA 24060.

MACGUFFIN POETRY CONTEST. Prizes of $500, $200, $100. Submit 5 unpublished poems. $15 reading fee. Deadline: submit between April 1 and May 30 only. *The MacGuffin* Poetry Contest, Schoolcraft College, Liberal Arts Building, 18600 Haggerty Road, Livonia, MI 48152 .

MARBLE FAWN POETRY COMPETITION. For a poem of any length. The prize: $750. $25 entry fee; April 1 deadline. Pirate's Alley Faulkner Society, Poetry Contest, 632 Pirate's Alley, New Orleans, LA 70116.

MARIE-LOUISE D'ESTERNAUX SONNET AWARD. Write for complete guidelines including deadlines and entry/reading fees: The Brooklyn Poetry Circle, Marie-Loui se D'Esternaux Contest, 2550 Independence Ave., #3U, Bronx, NY 10463.

MARY SCHEIRMAN POETRY AWARD. For a poem of up to 60 lines. Various themes; write for guidelines. Submitted poems may have been previously published. $500 first prize; runner-up awards of tuition to writer's conference. $10 reading fee (1-2 poems); July 1 deadline. Marya Scheirman Poetry Award, Coos Bay Writers Workshop, P.O. Box 4022, Coos Bay, OR 97420.

MASTERS LITERARY AWARD. Includes poetry. Three honorable mention awards and yearly $1,000 grand prize. Previously published poems acceptable. $10 entry fee. Editor, Masters Literary Awards, Center Press, Box 16452, Encino, CA 91416-6452.

MAURICE ENGLISH POETRY AWARD. Write for complete guidelines including deadlines and entry/reading fees: Maurice English

Foundation for Poetry, 2222 Rittenhouse Square, Philadelphia, PA 19103-5505.

MEDICINAL PURPOSES LITERARY REVIEW POETRY CONTEST.$100 first prize. For a poem between six and 16 lines. $5 entry fee covers up to 3 poems; no deadline listed. Send for guidelines: Contest, Poet to Poet, c/o Catterson, 86-37 120 St., #2D, Richmond Hill, NY 11418. ok

THE MILTON DORFMAN POETRY PRIZE. The prizes: $500, $200, $100. November 1 deadline. The Milton Dorfman Poetry Prize, Rome Art & Community Center, 308 W. Bloomfield St., Rome, NY 13440.

◆●MONTANA ARTS COUNCIL INDIVIDUAL ARTISTS GRANT. Biennial odd-numbered years. Including poets. *Montana residency at least one year.* The prize: 3 grants. Fall deadline. Montana Arts Council, 316 N. Park Ave, #252, Box 202201, Helena, MT 59620.

◆MINNESOTA TRAVEL AND STUDY GRANT PROGRAM. Including poetry writing projects. *For 3 writers residing in Minneapolis/St. Paul and 5 writers living elsewhere in the state.* The prizes: $540-$5,000. March deadline. Jerome Foundation, 125 Park Square Court, 400 Sibley St., St. Paul, MN 55101-1928.

MISSISSIPPI VALLEY POETRY CONTEST. Write for complete guidelines including deadlines and entry/reading fees: Mississippi Valley Poetry Contest, PO Box 3188, Rock Island, IL 61204.

MISSOURI REVIEW EDITORS' PRIZE Contest. Includes poetry. Prize of $750 and publication in magazine. Send up to 10 pages of poetry; $15 reading fee includes subscription. Send to: *The Missouri Review* Editors' Prize, 1507 Hillcrest Hall, Columbia, MO 65211.

M.O.O.N. MAGAZINE FINISH THIS POEM CONTEST. Prize for completing a poem; editors supply first three lines. Prize of $50, $25. $5 entry fee first poem, $1 each additional poem; Feb. 28 deadline. M.O.O.N. magazine, 8024 Cooper Road, Kenosha, WI 53142.

THE MUDFISH POETRY PRIZE. $500 prize and publication in magazine. $7 reading fee covers up to three poems; $2 each additional; write for current deadline. Mudfish Poetry Prize, *Mudfish*, 184 Franklin Street, New York, NY 10013.

NANCY BYRD TURNER MEMORIAL PRIZE. For a sonnet. The prizes: $50, $30, $20. January 15 deadline. Nancy Byrd Turner Memorial Prize, The Poetry Society of Virginia, 4712 Old Dominion Dr., Lynchburg, VA 24503.

NATIONAL ENDOWMENT FOR THE ARTS CREATIVE WRITING FELLOWSHIPS. Odd numbered years for poetry including translations ('97, 99, 2001,). For writing, research and travel. The prize: $20,000. Deadline for next poetry award (to be presented in 1999) sometime in 1998. National Endowment for the Arts, 1100 Pennsylvania Ave., NW, Washington DC 20505-0001.

NATIONAL FEDERATION OF STATE POETRY SOCIETIES ANNUAL POETRY CONTEST. The prizes: 50 contest prizes, $10-$1,500. March 15 deadline. National Federation of State Poetry Societies, 1206 13 Ave. SE, St. Cloud MN 56304.

NATIONAL POET HUNT. Prizes of $500, $250, $100. Send 5 unpublished poems. $15 reading fee; submit between April 1 and May 3. Send for complete guidelines. Poet Hunt, Liberal Arts Building, Schoolcraft College, 18600 Haggerty Road, Livonia, Michigan 48152.

Prize Competitions *for Poets*

NATIONAL POETRY COMPETITION. Cash prizes of $1,000, $750, $500, $250, $100, $50 and publication in anthology. Blind competition; entry form required. Submit up to 10 poems, 32-line limit each poem. Unpublished poetry only. Reading fee, $2 first poem, $1 each poem thereafter; March 31 deadline. The Chester H. Jones Foundation, PO Box 498 Chardon, OH 44024.

NATIONAL PRIZE IN POETRY AND FICTION. Includes poetry. $1,000 cash prize and publication in literary magazine, *The Michigan Quarterly Review*. Submit up to three poems. $10 reading fee. March 1 deadline. National Prize in Poetry and Fiction, The Loft, Pratt Community Center, 66 Malcom Avenue S.E., Minneapolis, MN 55414.

THE NEBRASKA REVIEW AWARDS . Includes poetry.. $500 prize, publication For a poem or group of poems, total length not to exceed 5 poems or 6 pages. Reading fee $9. Deadline November 30. Poetry Prize, *Nebraska Review*, University of Nebraska, Omaha, Nebraska 68182.

NEGATIVE CAPABILITY POETRY AND SHORT FICTION AWARDS. Prize of $1,000 and publication. $10 entry fee; January 15 deadline. *Negative Capability*, Poetry and Short Fiction Awards, 62 Ridgelawn Drive East, Mobile, AL 36608.

NEW LETTERS LITERARY AWARDS . Includes poetry. $750 prize plus magazine publication. Submit group of 3-6 poems. $10 reading fee. May 15 deadline. *New Letters*, University of Missouri-Kansas City, 5100 Rockhill Road, Kansas City, MO 64110.

NEW MILLENNIUM AWARDS. $500 prize for poetry. Send up to five poems. $10 reading fee (includes subscription to magazine); December 1 deadline. New Millenium Writings, P.O. Box 40987, Nashville, TN 37204.

NEW ENGLAND WRITERS FREE VERSE CONTEST. Write for complete guidelines including deadlines and entry/reading fees to: Dr. Frank Anthony, New England Writers Contest, 151 Main Street, PO Box 483, Windsor, VT 05089-0483.

NEW RENAISSANCE POETRY AWARD. $250, $125, $50, $20 plus publication. All submissions made to the magazine are eligible for the award, but all must pay the reading fee before any work is considered. Send manuscript with SASE and entry fee. Entry fees: for current subscribers, $10; for non-subscibers, $15 (includes current issue plus back issues.) Submit January through May, 1997. Inquire for other deadlines. Send to: Louise T. Reynolds,Editor-in-Chuief, *new renaissance*, 26 Heath Road #11, Arlington, MA 02174.

NEW WRITING AWARD. For new writing by new writers. Odd numbered years. Includes poetry. The prize: $8,000. March 1 deadline.New Writing Award, New Writing, Box 1812, Amherst, NY 14226-7812.

NEWPORT COMMUNITY WRITERS ASSOCIATION poetry competition. $250 prize plus tuition to writers conference. Submit 3 photocopies of poem(s) of any length or subject matter, plus cover sheet. Is blind competition. $10 reading fee; June 1 deadline. Community Writers Association, P.O. Box 12, Newport, RI 02840.

◆NORTH AMERICAN NATIVE AUTHORS FIRST BOOK AWARDS. Write for complete guidelines including deadlines and entry/reading fees to: Native Writers Circle of the Americas College of Arts and Sciences University of Oklahoma Norman, OK 73019.

NORTH AMERICAN OPEN POETRY CONTEST. Write for complete guidelines including deadlines and entry/reading fees to: National Library of Poetry, 11419 Cronridge Drive, PO Box 704-YR, Owings Mills, MD 21117.

Prize Competitions *for Poets*

OH SUSANNA PRESS writing contest. Includes poetry. Is thematic contest. Cash prizes and publication in anthology. $2 reading fee; no deadline listed. Oh Susanna Press, 2312 Colchester Drive, Edmond, OK 73034.

OHIOANA POETRY AWARD. Write for complete guidelines including deadlines and entry/reading fees to: Ohioana Library Association, 65 South Front St., #1105, Columbus, OH 43215

OPEN VOICE AWARDS. Includes poetry. $500 Prize and public reading. Submit up to 10 pages of poetry. Entry fee $10; December 31 deadline. The Writer's Voice, 5 West 63 Street, New York, NY 10023.

◆●OREGON ARTS COMMISSION INDIVIDUAL ARTISTS FELLOWSHIPS. Biennial, even-numbered years. Includes poetry. *For writers residing in Oregon for at least one year*, to help them in their careers. The prize: $3,000. Write for 1998 deadlines and new guidelines. Oregon Arts Commission, 775 Summer St. Southeast, Salem, OR 97310.

OVAL MAGAZINE POETRY CONTEST. $125 first prize, $75 second prize, honorable mention awards. Submit up to 9 poems. $9 entry fee; May 15 deadline. Contest, *Oval Magazine*, 22 Douglass Street, Brooklyn, NY 11231.

P.L.C. INTERNATIONAL POETRY AWARDS (I). Open to U.S. poets every third year (1996,1999, etc.), for an unpublished poem. The prizes: $1,000, $500. Submit one or more poems, any length. Deadline to be announced in 1998-9. Abbey National, P.L.C. International Poetry Awards, Cleveland Arms Building, 4-E, 205 W. 95th St., New York, NY 10025-6383.

P.L.C. International Poetry Awards (II). Open to U.S. poets every third year (1996,1999, etc.), for "an unpublished poem with a multi-cultural and international viewpoint." The prize: $750 and possible publication. Submit one or more poems, any length. Deadline to be announced in 1998-9. Abbey National, P.L.C. International Poetry Awards, Cleveland Arms Building, 4-E, 205 W. 95th St., New York, NY 10025-6383.

PABLO NERUDA PRIZE FOR POETRY. For a single longpoem, series of related poems, or selection of short poems; length: 1,000 word minimum, 1,800 word maximum. Poetry should be unpublished. Submit two copies. Is blind competition. Prizes of $1,000, $500 and publication in magazine. $15 entry fee. April 15 deadline. Write for complete details. *Nimrod International Journal of Prose and Poetry*, University of Tulsa, 600 South College Avenue, Tulsa, OK 74104.

PAINTED BRIDE QUARTERLY POETRY CONTEST. Prizes of $50, $25, and $15; publication in magazine. $3 reading fee. Deadline June 30. *Painted Bride Quarterly*, c/o Painted Bride Art Center, 230 Bine Street, Philadelphia, PA 19106.

PARALLEL POETRY CONTEST. The prizes: $500 and publication in the *Bellingham Review*, $250 second, $100 third, and publication. $5 per poem entry fee; November 30 deadline. Parallel Poetry Contest, The Sign Post Press, 9053 Mail Stop, Bellingham, WA 98225.

◆PASSAGER POETRY CONTEST. *For poets age 50 or more.* $500 prize and publication in magazine. Submit five poems 30 lines or less. Include short biography. $5 reading fee; March 15 deadline. Passager Poetry Contest, School of Communications Design, University of Baltimore, 1420 North Charles Street, Baltimore, MD 21201.

PAUMANOK POETRY AWARDS. First prize of $1,000 and an all-expense paid reading. Two Second Prize awards of $500 and expenses for a reading. Deadline: September 15. Send cover letter, one paragraph bio, one to five of your best poems (no more than 10 pages total). $15 entry fee. Dr. Margery Brown,

Director, Visiting Writers Program, Knapp Hall, SUNY-Farmingdale, Farmingdale, NY 11735.

PENUMBRA POETRY COMPETITION. Various competitions for short poetry and haiku. Write for guidelines and additional requirements. June 30 deadline. Penumbra Poetry Contest, P.O. Box 15995, Tallahassee, FL 32317-5995.

PEREGRINE PRIZE Includes poetry. For a poem of less than 70 lines. $500 prize and publication. Send for guidelines before submitting. $10 reading fee; April 17 deadline. Peregrine Prize, P.O. Box 1076, Amherst, MA 01004.

PETERLOO POETS OPEN POETRY COMPETITION. For a poem of 40 lines or less. Grand prize 4,000 British pounds; 2,100 British pounds in other prizes. Send SAE with international reply coupon for required entry form. 4 pound reading fee per poem; March 1 deadline (foreign currency or checks not accepted). Send for guidelines: Peterloo Poetry Competition, 2 Kelly Gardens, Calstock, Cornwall PL18 9SA, United Kingdom.

◆●PENNSYLVANIA COUNCIL ON THE ARTS LITERATURE PROGRAM. Fellowships to poets on the odd years, fiction writers on the even years. *For writers with 2 years residency in the state.* The prizes: $5,000-$10,000 to as many as 13 writers per year. August 1 deadline. Pennsylvania Council on the Arts, 216 Finance Building, Harrisburg, PA 17120.

THE PHYLLIS SMART YOUNG PRIZE IN POETRY. For the best group of three poems. $500 prize and magazine publication. Submit only during September. $3 reading fee; September 30 deadline. Phyllis Smart Young Prize, *The Madison Review*, English Department, University of Wisconsin-Madison, 600 North Park Street, Madison, WI 53706.

PITTENBRUACH PRESS POETRY CONTEST. Is thematic: write for themes. Prizes of $100, $75, $50 plus publication. Send short bio note. No fee; February 1 deadline. Pittenbruach Press, 15 Walnut Street, P.O. Box 553, Northampton, MA 01061.

PLUM REVIEW POETRY CONTEST. Prize of $500 plus publication. Submit up to 3 poems in any length. $5.00 reading fee; February 28 deadline. Poetry contest, *The Plum Review*, P.O. Box 1347, Philadelphia, PA 19105.

POETRY IN PRINT prize. Includes poetry. Submit poems, 30 lines maximum. The prize: $500. $5 entry fee; August 31 deadline. *Poetry in Print*, Box 30981, Albuquerque, NM 87109-0981.

POETRY MAGAZINE AWARDS. A variety of awards and prizes in oetry; various forms. Send for complete guidelines including deadlines and rntry/ reading fees. *Poetry*, 60 West Walton Street, Chicago, IL 60610.

POETRY SOCIETY OF MICHIGAN CONTEST. The prizes: $75, $35 in six categories, publication in *PSM Peninsula Poets* and reading at PSM meeting. $2 entry fee per poem. PSM Contest, 60 Benton Rd., Saginaw, MI 48602.

QUINCY WRITERS GUILD ANNUAL CREATIVE WRITING CONTEST. Including poetry. The prizes: 1st, 2nd, 3rd, amounts vary. April 15 deadline. Quincy Writers Guild Annual Creative Writing Contest, Quincy Writers Guild, Box 112, Natalie Miller Rotunda, Quincy, IL, 62306-0112.

RAINMAKER AWARDS IN POETRY. Prizes of $500, $300, and $100. Submit up to three poems. $8 reading fee (includes subscription). January 1 deadline. Rainmaker Awards in Poetry, *Zone 3*, Austin Peay State University, P0 Box 4565, Clarksville, TN 37044.

RAMBUNCTIOUS REVIEW POETRY CONTEST. For poem on a particular theme chosen by the editors. Prizes of $100, $75, $50 and publication. Submit up to three poems, not to exceed

100 lines each. $2 entry fee per poem; November 17 deadline. *Rambunctious Review*, 1221 West Pratt Boulevard, Chicago, IL 60626.

RANDALL JARRELL POETRY PRIZE. For an unpublished poem in any genre. $500 prize plus magazine publication. Submit up to three poems, in total not more than ten pages in length. $5 reading fee; November 1 deadline. The North Carolina Writers' Network, PO Box 954, Carrboro, NC 27510.

RATTLE poetry contest. For poem of less than 36 lines, which includes the word "rattle." Prize: publication and subscription. Send for guidelines. *Rattle* magazine, 13440 Ventura Blvd., Suite 200, Sherman Oaks, CA 91423.

◆●RHODE ISLAND STATE COUNCIL ON THE ARTS. Biennial awards to *poets and fiction writers who are residents of Rhode Island for at least one year prior to April 1*. Write for complete guidelines including deadlines and entry/reading fees to: Rhode Island State Council on the Arts, 95 Cedar St., #103, Providence, RI 02903.

RHYME TIME WRITING COMPETITION. Including poetry. The prize: cash. November 1 deadline. Rhyme Time Writing Competition, *Rhyme Time*, Box 2907, Decatur, IL 62524.

RIVER CITY WRITING AWARDS IN FICTION. Write for complete guidelines including deadlines and entry/reading fees to: Contest Editor, *River City*, Department of English, The University of Memphis, Memphis, TN 38152.

RIVER STYX MAGAZINE INTERNATIONAL POETRY CONTEST. Is blind competition. Send up to three poems. $15 reading fee; May 31 deadline. *River Styx* magazine, 3207 Washington Street, St. Louis, MO 63103.

ROBERT FRANCIS MEMORIAL PRIZE. $250 prize and magazine

publication. For previously unpublished poems Reading fee, $2 per poem. October 31 deadline. *Mockingbird RFM*, P.O. Box 761, Davis, CA 95617.

◆ROBERT H. WINNER MEMORIAL AWARD. *Presented to a poet over 40 years of age who has published no more than one full-length volume of poetry.* Prize of $2,500. Submit manuscript of up to ten poems (not to exceed 20 pages). $5 entry fee, nonmembers; December 22 deadline. Write for complete guidelines: Robert H. Winner Memorial Award, Poetry Society of America, 15 Gramercy Park, New York, NY 10003.

ROBERT PENN WARREN AWARDS. For unpublished, original free verse of 30 lines or less. Prizes of $200, $100, $50 plus publication in magazine. Entry fee $5 for three poems. June 15 deadline. Robert Penn Warren Awards, P.O. Box 483, Windsor, VT 05089.

ROBERT PENN WARREN POETRY PRIZE. Prizes of $500, $300, $200 plus magazine publication. Submit 1-3 unpublished poems, line limit less than 100 lines each. $14 reading fee. March 15 deadline. Robert Penn Warren Poetry Prize, *Cumberland Poetry Review*, P.O. Box 120128, Acklen Station, Nashville, TN 37212.

ROBINSON JEFFERS PRIZE. $500 prize for best poem. Submit poems up to three pages in length. $10 reading fee covers up to three poems, $15 for up to six; March 1 deadline. Robinson Jeffers Prize, P.O Box 223240, Carmel, CA 93922.

ROCK RIVER POETRY CONTEST. The prizes: $100, $50, $25, publication and reading. $2 entry fee per poem. May 2 deadline. Rock River Poetry Contest, Rockford Art Museum, 711 N. Main St., Rockford, IL 61103.

ROCKY MOUNTAIN ARTIST'S/ECCENTRIC BOOK COMPETITION. Write

for complete guidelines including deadlines and entry/reading fees to: Tom Trusky, Editor, Hemingway Western Studies Center, Boise State University, Boise, ID 83725.

RONALD H. BAYES POETRY PRIZE. For a single poem of less than 5 single-spaced pages. $500 prize; $5 reading fee. April 1 deadline. Ronald H. Bayes Poetry Prize, *Sandhills Review*, 2200 Airport Road, Pinehurst, NC 28374.

RUTH CABLE MEMORIAL PRIZE FOR POETRY. $500 first prize; honorable mentions of $50; publication in magazine. Submit 3 or more poems up to 50 lines in length. Entry fee $8 for 3 poems, $3 each additional poem. March 31 (postmark) deadline. Electric Literary Forum, Poetry Competition, P.O. Box 392, Tonawanda, NY 14150.

SALT HILL JOURNAL POETRY PRIZE. $500 first prize, $100 second prize, honorable mentions, plus magazine publication. Submit 3 unpublished poems; no restrictions on length. $5 entry fee; May 1 deadline. *Salt Hill Journal*, English Department, 401 Hall of Languages, Syracuse University, Syracuse, NY 13244.

SAN JOSE CENTER POETRY COMPETITION. $500 prize. For a poem of any length. Reading fee $10 for submission of up to three poems; additional poems, $3 each. March 1 deadline. San Jose Center for Poetry and Literature, P.O. Box 221847, Carmel, CA 93922.

SAND RIVER CONTEST FOR POETRY IN TRADITIONAL FIXED FORMS. Write for complete guidelines including deadlines and entry/reading fees to: The Editors, Sand River Poetry Contest, TDM Press, USC-Aiken, 171 University Parkway, Aiken, SC 29801.

SANDBURG-LIVESAY ANTHOLOGY poetry contest. For individual poems (80 lines or less) in the tradition of Carl Sandburg and Dorothy Livesay. $100 prize plus publication in anthology. $8 reading fee; October 31 deadline. Sandburg-Livesay Anthology Contest, c/o Unfinished Monument Press, P.O. Box 4279, Pittsburg, PA 15203.

SARA HENDERSON HAY PRIZE FOR POETRY. Write for complete guidelines including deadlines and entry/reading fees to: *The Pittsburgh Quarterly*, 36 Haberman Avenue, Pittsburgh, PA 15211-2144.

SCARS PUBLICATIONS CALENDAR POETRY CONTEST. Publication as part of wall calendar; winning entries constitute one month of calendar. Up to 40 line poem. Entry fee $10. Ongoing deadline. Scars Publications, 2543 North Kimball, Chicago, IL 60647.

SHENANDOAH VALLEY WRITERS' GUILD CREATIVE WRITING CONTEST. Includes poetry. For amateur and semi-professional writers. The prize: $25. March 15 deadline. Creative Writing Contest, Shenandoah Valley Writers Guild, Lord Fairfax Community College, Box 47, Middletown, VA 22645.

THE SHORT GRAIN WRITING CONTEST annually offers a $500 first prize, a $300 second prize, and a $200 third prize in each of three categories: "Postcard Story," a work of fiction of up to 500 words; "Prose Poem," a lyric poem written as a prose paragraph of up to 500 words. Winning works will be published in *Grain*. $20 entry fee. Deadline: January 31. *Grain* magazine, Box 1154, Regina, Saskatchewan S4P 3B4, Canada.

SIDNEY BECHET CENTENNIAL POETRY PRIZE. Poetry about the lengendary New Orleans jazzman. The prize: $250 and publication. April 1 deadline. Rod Jellema, English Dept., University of Maryland, 4109 Susquehanna, College Park, MD 20742.

Prize Competitions *for Poets*

SILVER WINGS POETRY CONTEST. Write for complete guidelines including deadlines and entry/reading fees to: Silver Wings, PO Box 1000, Pearblossom, CA 93553.

SIMI VALLEY BRANCH OF THE NATIONAL LEAGUE OF AMERICAN PEN WOMEN CONTEST. Prizes of $100. Poetry (50 line maximum). Entry fees are $3 each poem. Postmark deadline: July 30. For complete rules send a SASE to: NLAPW-SVB Contest Rules, P.O. Box 1485, Simi Valley, Ca 93062.

SONORA REVIEW POETRY CONTEST. Publication in magazine, $500 prize. Entry fee of $10 covers up to four poems. July 1 deadline. *Sonora Review*, c/o Department of English, University of Arizona, Tucson, AZ 85721.

SOPHOMORE JINX "BEGINNER'S LUCK" POETRY CONTEST. Write for complete guidelines, deadlines and fees, entry forms to: "Beginner's Luck" Poetry Contest, *Sophomore Jinx*, PO Box 770728, Woodside, NY 1137.

SOUTHERN PRIZE FOR POETRY. $600 first prize. Prize winner and top finalists published in the Anthology. Submit three poems, no restrictions on theme or style. $10 entry fee. May 30 deadline. *The Southern Anthology*, 2851 Johnston St., Lafayette, LA 70501.

SOUTHWEST WRITERS WORKSHOP CONTEST. Write for complete guidelines, deadlines and fees, entry forms to: SWW Contest, Southwest Writers Workshop, 1338 Wyoming Blvd., N.E., Suite B, Albuquerque, NM 87112.

◆SOUTHWEST REVIEW/MARGARET L. HARTLEY AWARD. Including poetry. *For minority writers.* The prize: $250. Year-round submissions. *Southwest Review* Awards, Margaret L. Hartley Award, Box 374, 307 Fondren Library W., Southern Methodist University, Dallas, TX 75275-0374.

THE SOW'S EAR POETRY PRIZE. For a single poem. The prizes: $500, $100, $50. September-October submission dates. *The Sow's Ear* Poetry Prize, *The Sow's Ear Poetry Journal*, 10575 Pleasant View Dr., Abingdon, VA 24211-6827.

SPARROWGRASS POETRY CONTEST. Write for complete guidelines including deadlines and entry/reading fees to: Sparrowgrass Poetry Forum, 88203 Diamond Street, Sistersville, WV 26175

SPOON RIVER POETRY REVIEW EDITORS PRIZE. $500 and magazine publication. Submit 3 poems, not to exceed 10 pages in toto. $15 reading fee. May 1 deadline. Editors Prize, *Spoon River Poetry Review*, 4240 English Department, Illinois State University, Normal, IL 61790.

STAND MAGAZINE POETRY COMPETITION. For original poem in English to 500 lines. Prizes of L1,500; L500; L250; L150; L100; 20 runner-up awards of books and subscription to magazine. Top winners receive publication in magazine. Donation (the magazine is a registered charity) of at least L3.50 (US $7) required. Two copies of each poem required. Deadline June 30. Entry form required. Send SASE and two international reply coupons to *Stand Magazine*, 179 Wingrove Road, Newcastle Upon Tyne NE4 9DA, England.

STANLEY JOSEPH AWARD. Includes poetry. For a poem not to exceed 30 lines in length. $100 prize. Submit up to five poems. $5 reading fee; March 1 deadline. Write Stanley Joseph Award, c/o *Coracle*, 1516 Euclid Ave., Berkeley, CA 94708.

STEPHEN LEACOCK POETRY AWARDS. Write for complete guidelines including deadlines and entry/reading fees to: Orillia International Poetry Festival, PO Box 2307, Orillia, Ontario, Canada L3V 6S2.

STROUSSE AWARD. Write for complete guidelines including deadlines and entry/reading fees to: *Prairie Schooner*, 201

Andrews Hall, University of Nebraska, Lincoln, NE 68588-0334.

SUE SANIEL ELKIND POETRY CONTEST. Write for complete guidelines including deadlines and entry/reading fees to: *Kalliope*, Sue Saniel Elkind Poetry Contest, FCCJ, 3939 Roosevelt Blvd., Jacksonville, FL 32205.

TAPROOT WRITER'S WORKSHOP INC. WRITING CONTEST. Includes poetry. Cash prizes plus publication in anthology. December 31 deadline. Write for guidelines: Taproot Writer's Workshop Inc., Taproot, 302 Park Road, Ambridge, PA 15003.

TORONTO ARTS AWARDS. Including poetry. The prize: commemorative art piece, $2,500 value. Write for complete guidelines including deadlines and entry/reading fees to Toronto Arts Awards, Arts Foundation of Greater Toronto, 40 Richmond St. W., Toronto M5V 2T2 Canada.

●VERMONT COUNCIL ON THE ARTS GRANTS. Including poets. The prize: opportunity grants up to $3,000 for collaborative projects involving a poet and an organization or school, and Professional Development grants of $250 to $400 to poets for specific projects. January 7 deadline for projects occurring March 15-August 31 and April 7 deadline for projects occurring June 15-August 31.

VERVE JOURNAL POETRY CONTEST. Prizes of $100, $50, $25, plus publication. Sponsors two contests a year. $2 entry fee; write for deadlines and contest guidelines. Verve Poetry Contest, P.O. Box 3205, Simi Valley, CA 93093.

VIRGINIA FAULKNER AWARD FOR EXCELLENCE IN WRITING. Including poetry. The prize: $1,000. May 1-31 submission dates. Virginia Faulkner Award for Excellence in Writing, *Prairie Schooner*, University of Nebraska, 201 Andrews, Lincoln, NE 68588-0334.

THE WHISKEY ISLAND POETRY AND FICTIONCONTEST. Prizes of $300; $200;$100. Submit 5-10 pages of poetry. Is blind competition.. $10 entry fee; January 31 deadline. Send for guidelines to: Whiskey Island Contest, English Department, Cleveland State University, Cleveland, OH 44115.

THE WILDWOOD PRIZE IN POETRY. For a poem of less than 100 lines. Prize: $500 and magazine publication. Submit 1-3 poems. $5 Reading fee; Submit between September 30-November 30. Write for guidelines: Wildwood Prize, Harrisburg Area Community Col. Rose Lehrman Arts Ctr., 213-E, 1 HACC Drive, Harrisburg, PA 17110.

◆WRITERS AT WORK POETRY FELLOWSHIP COMPETITION. *For a poet who has not yet published a book-length work.* Is blind competition. Prizes of $1,500 and $500 plus publication in the literary magazine *Quarterly West,* featured reading, and tuition to writer's conference. Submit up to six poems, 10 page total maximum. $12 reading fee. March 15 deadline.Writers At Work Competition, P.O. Bix 1146, Centerville, UT 84014.

WRITER'S DIGEST AWARDS. Includes poetry. For an original poem of up to 32 lines. Variety of cash and other prizes. $7 entry fee; write for deadlines and complete guidelines and required entry form. Writer's Digest Writing Competition, Writer's Digest, 1507 Dana Ave., Cincinnati, OH 45207.

VERVE POETRY CONTEST(S). For single poem. First prize $100 plus publication; 2nd, $50; 3rd, $25. $2 reading fee per poem; April 1 and October 1 deadlines. *Verve* journal, PO Box 3205, Simi Valley, CA 93093.

◆VILLA MONTALVO BIENNIAL POETRY COMPETITION. *Open only to residents of California, Oregon, Washington, or Nevada.* First prize of $1,000 and 30-day residence at artists' retreat; other prizes of $500, $300. Write for deadlines and guidelines to Villa Montalvo Biennial Poetry Competition, Villa Montalvo

Artist Rersidency Program, P.O. Box 158, Saratoga, CA 95071.

WHETSTONE PRIZE. $500 prize. For the best poetry, fiction, or creative non-fiction published annually in *Whetstone* literary magazine. September 1 deadline. Write for complete information and guidelines. The Whetstone Prize, *Whetstone*, Barrington Area Arts Council, P.O. Box 1266, Barrington, IL 60011.

WHITE RABBIT POETRY CONTEST. Prizes of $100, $50, $25, honorable mentions; publication in magazine. $5 entry fee first poem, $2 each additional. March 31 deadline. *Harbinger* magazine, P.O. Box U-1030, USAL, Mobile, AL 36688.

WILLOW SPRINGS POETRY CONTEST. Prizes of $200 and $125; publication in magazine. January 31 deadline. *Willow Springs* magazine, 526 Fifth Street, MS-1, Eastern Washington University, Cheney, WA 99004

WORLD FANTASY AWARDS ADMINISTRATION. Including poetry. The prize: trophy. July 31 deadline. World Fantasy Awards Administration, 5 Winding Brook Dr., #1B, Guilderland, NY 12084.

WRITE WAY POETRY CONTESTS . Write for complete guidelines including deadlines and entry/reading fees to: Ann Larberg, Editor, 810 Overhill Road, DeLand, FL 32720- 1440.

THE WRITERS COMMUNITY CONTEST. Including poetry. For mid-career writers. Biannual award. The prize: $6,000 and semester long residency, YMCA-based literary arts centers nationwide. The Writers Community, National Writers Voice Project, 5 W. 63 St., New York, NY 10023.

WRITER'S DIGEST WRITING COMPETITION. Including poetry. The grand prize: expense-paid trip to New York, lunch with four editors or agents, cash, reference books, word processing programs. Write for complete guidelines including deadlines and entry/reading fees to: *Writer's Digest* Writing Competition, *Writer's Digest*, 1507 Dana Ave., Cincinnati, OH 45207.

WRITERS JOURNAL SEMI-ANNUAL POETRY CONTEST. The prizes: $25, $15, $10. April 15 and November 15 deadlines. *Writers Journal* Semi-Annual Poetry Contest, Minnesota Ink, 27 Empire Dr., St. Paul, MN 55103.

WRITERS OF KERN CONTEST. Including poetry. The prizes: $50, $35, $25. presented at To Get Ink Writers Conference. July 15 deadline. Writers of Kern, Box 6694, Bakersfield, CA 93386-6694.

◆●WYOMING COUNCIL ON THE ARTS LITERARY FELLOWSHIPS. Including poetry. *For two-year Wyoming residents eighteen years of age or older as of July 15.* The prizes: four $2,000 fellowships, a $1,000 Neltje Blanchan Literary Award for nature-inspired writing, the $1,000 Frank Nelson Doubleday Award for a woman writer. Submit up to 10 pages of unpublished poetry. June 1 deadline. Wyoming Council on the Arts, 230 Capitol Ave., Cheyenne, WY 82002.

YEATS POETRY PRIZE. $100 1st place, $75 2nd place. Honorable Mentions. Poem should not exceed 50 lines. Reading fee $6 for 1st poem, $4 per additional poem. Entries must be received by March 15. Mail to: W. B. Yeats Society of NY, National Arts Club, 15 Gramercy Park South., New York, NY 10003.

ZUZU'S PETALS POETRY CONTEST. The prize: 40% of proceeds from entry fees. March 1, June 1, December 1 deadlines. Zuzu's Petals Poetry Contest, Box 4476, Allentown, PA 18105.

BIBLIOGRAPHY

Poets & Writers Magazine. 6 issues/year; subscription $19.95/year. Published by Poets & Writers Inc., 72 Spring Street, New York, NY 10012. This periodical has perhaps the most complete listings of competitions issue-by-issue of any periodical, in their "Grants and Awards" and "Deadlines" sections, as well as many classified and space adds which are announcements of contests. The magazine itself is heavily oriented toward university writing programs and writers who are in academe.

Poetry Flash. 1450 Fourth Street #4, Berkeley, CA 94710. 9 issues/year; $16/year An interesting magazine, an amalgam of information, reviews, interviews calendar events and commentary, especially about the California poetry/literary scene. Their information section contains announcements of many contests and competitions.

Small Press Review. 12 issues/year. Subscription $25 year to individuals, $31 year to institutions. Published by Dustbooks, Box 100, Paradise, California 95967. The "news & notes" column is an excellent source of informaion about new and ongoing contests, especially for those publications which are not university-based.

The SPR publishes many reviews, both of small press books and, more recently, of small literary magazines and periodicals.

The reader is also directed to THE INTERNATIONAL DIRECTORY OF LITTLE MAGAZINES AND SMALL PRESSES, an annual reference book which is the oldest and moast comprehensive listing of small press operations in existence. Of particular interest to the poet is the Dustbook volume DIRECTORY OF POETRY PUBLISHERS (same address).

The Writer. 12/year; Subscription $28/year Published by The Writer, Inc., 120 Boyleston Street, Boston, MA 02116. This monthly magazine has a "Prize Offers" column which gives informationon a variety of contests for poetry, fiction, and nonfiction/screenwriting.

Writer's Digest. 12 issues/year; subscription $27/year. Published by F&W Publications, Inc., 1507 Dana Avenue, Cincinnati, OH 45207. *Writer's Digest* is an excellent source of information and advice for writers, especially those who are just beginning. This magazine's "The Markets" column often has complete information on various poetry and other contests. The "Poetry" column also may occasionally have information on prizes and competitions. The classified ad section called "Writer's Mart," as well as ads throughout the magazine, is a popular place for contests to announce themselves and call for submissions. However, some of these contests are anthologies which may require purchase of a copy of the antholgy for inclusion.

LITERARY MARKET PLACE. Published by R.R. Bowker Co., 121 Chanlon Road, New Providence, NJ 07974. This weighty and expensive reference work contains a useful section of general prizes and awards of all kinds, though it is not comprehensive. Most libraries have the LMP, as it is generally known, in the reference section.

POET'S MARKET. Published by F&W Publications, Inc., 1507 Dana Avenue, Cincinnati, OH 45207. As with *Writer's Digest*, this annual reference book is a good source of information and advice for writers, especially beginners. The volume has a short section on poetry contests and competitions of various kinds, with complete details.

INDEX OF CONTESTS

Prize Competitions *for Poets*

Prize Competitions *for Poets*

Prize Competitions *for Poets*

Prize Competitions *for Poets*

INDEX OF RESTRICTED CONTESTS

Prize Competitions *for Poets*

INDEX OF SPONSORING PUBLISHERS AND ORGANIZATIONS

Prize Competitions *for Poets*